DONAL SKEHAN
KITCHEN HERO

DONAL SKEHAN
KITCHEN HERO

Bringing Cooking Back Home!

Collins

CONTENTS

INTRODUCTION

I am a home cook and I'm here to show you how to be a kitchen hero!

I've come to the conclusion that if you have confidence in the kitchen, you can cook absolutely anything. And I mean ANYTHING. The beauty of this little theory is that it can be applied to anybody. I'm talking about the toast-burning gang, the squeamish can't-touch-raw-chicken folk, and the won't-boil-an-egg brigade! My advice is this: first of all, do not under any circumstances give up, because once you've accepted your burnt chicken or rubbery steak as valuable experience and are ready to move on, that is when you are well on your way.

I learned to cook by trying different recipes from cookbooks over the years, which helped me develop the confidence to get into the kitchen without guidance. Using just a few ingredients, I could soon create dishes which tasted good and also had people begging for the recipe. Look, I'm giving you the hard sell here and I know it can be quite daunting heading into the kitchen and cooking a meal for four if you haven't done it before, but I promise that if you can master at least three recipes from this cookbook (or any cookbook), you will not only impress yourself, you will want to master more and more. That's when it all starts to get interesting.

One of the funny things about the big world of All Things Food is that, generally speaking, once you're in, you're in for life. Soon you will find yourself dreaming about kitchen gadgets, stroking kitchen counters in showrooms (I like to think it isn't just me who does this!) and reading cookbooks in bed. If all of that hasn't happened just yet, prepare yourself,

it's coming! My aim for this book is to give you some great recipes that will become part of your everyday routine, recipes that appeal to all the home cooks out there. After all, the success of every good cook starts with what they make at home. Some people can be easily put off when they see chefs using a vast array of complex ingredients and techniques on TV, but as impressive as all that can be, it is quite easy to forget that the average house does not have a wide range of cooking implements or a store cupboard packed with exotic ingredients. Restaurant food may be exciting and inspiring, but it's simply not the type of food most people cook at home.

So, with all that in mind, it's time to get stuck in and explore the recipes in my book. They were all created with the home cook in mind, so I hope they inspire those of you who already cook every day, and also encourage those who have never cooked before. I want to give you the confidence to get into the kitchen and start bashing those pots and pans! To get started, fill your kitchen with the basic ingredients and spend a few quid on getting some essential kitchen equipment. Create a place where you want to experiment and have fun. Read cookbooks, trawl through food magazines, talk to food producers, or even go fishing. Visit markets, search for interesting ingredients, try things you haven't eaten before, travel to new places and, most importantly, love and share the food you eat. For me, nothing is more pleasing than seeing people enjoying something I have cooked for them.

So what are you waiting for? Get cooking!

DONAL SKEHAN

KITCHEN HERO ESSENTIALS

To really bring out the kitchen hero within, you first need to stock up on the basics. It doesn't matter what sort of kitchen you have – big or small, new or old – what really counts is how it's set up and that it functions for all your wants and needs. My mum always cursed her small kitchen and dreamed of an open-plan set-up with all the mod cons, rather than the galley she operated out of, where you couldn't swing a cat. But that never stopped her producing delicious meals every day while I was growing up. The truth is that every kitchen is different and it's all about creating something that works for you.

Essential Store-cupboard Ingredients

I am always banging on about a well-stocked kitchen, and the main reason is because I know that if I didn't have those ingredients to hand, I just wouldn't bother cooking. It's really not difficult to pack your cupboards with inspirational ingredients that will have you running to the kitchen in giddy excitement. (Or maybe that's just me!) Having a well-stocked store cupboard is the key to successful cooking. The list opposite is quite extensive, but have a read through and decide what you are most likely to use, or maybe choose a few recipes that you want to try, and make sure you pick up the essentials that you'll need for them.

BASICS

RICE

PASTA

NOODLES

BULGUR WHEAT

COUSCOUS

LENTILS: GREEN, RED AND BROWN

TINNED TOMATOES

TINNED BEANS

JARS OF TUNA IN OLIVE OIL
(NICER THAN TINNED)

OIL: OLIVE, SUNFLOWER,
VEGETABLE AND GROUNDNUT

VINEGAR: WHITE WINE,
RED WINE AND BALSAMIC

MUSTARD: ENGLISH, DIJON
AND WHOLEGRAIN

EGGS

PEANUT BUTTER

NUTS: WALNUTS, ALMONDS,
BRAZILS, HAZELNUTS, PEANUTS,
PECANS, PISTACHIOS AND PINE NUTS

SEEDS: PUMPKIN, SUNFLOWER,
SESAME AND POPPY

SPICES: PAPRIKA, CUMIN, CORIANDER,
CAYENNE PEPPER, CURRY POWDER,
TURMERIC, GROUND GINGER, GROUND
CINNAMON AND NUTMEG

CURRY PASTE

WORCESTERSHIRE SAUCE

TABASCO SAUCE

VEGETABLE BOUILLON POWDER

JAR OF SALSA

WHOLEMEAL TORTILLA WRAPS

HONEY

WINE: WHITE AND RED

FROZEN PUFF PASTRY

FROZEN PEAS

BAKING INGREDIENTS

FLOUR: PLAIN AND SELF-RAISING

CORNFLOUR

ACTIVE DRIED YEAST

BAKING POWDER

GOLDEN SYRUP

TREACLE

VANILLA EXTRACT

BUTTER

SUGAR: SOFT BROWN, DEMERARA, ICING,
CASTER AND GRANULATED

COCOA POWDER

CHOCOLATE: DARK, MILK,
WHITE AND CHIPS

CONDENSED MILK

JUMBO OAT FLAKES

ASIAN COOKING INGREDIENTS

SESAME OIL

RICE WINE

SOY SAUCE

FISH SAUCE (NAM PLA)

TERIYAKI SAUCE

OYSTER SAUCE

THAI SWEET CHILLI SAUCE

STAR ANISE

SZECHWAN PEPPERCORNS

Herbs in Pots

Growing herbs at home means you will always have a good supply to add to your recipes when you need them. Herbs such as rosemary, sage and thyme are hardy enough to keep you going throughout the year. Oregano, basil and mint tend to prefer the spring and summer months.

I'm often left with an overload of herbs, so rather than let them die during the winter, I like to find different ways to use them. You can dry thyme and oregano by cutting large bunches, shaking to remove any dirt or bugs and tying with a piece of string. Put in a warm, dry place and allow to dry out over a week, before popping in glass jars. To use, scrunch the bunches over tomato sauces or into salad dressings for a great aromatic kick. A tip for softer herbs like basil is to finely chop and mix with some good-quality olive oil, then pour the mixture into ice trays and pop in the freezer. You can stir these little herby cubes into sauces or I often defrost them and spread them over bread dough, along with a good sprinkling of sea salt, before baking it in the oven.

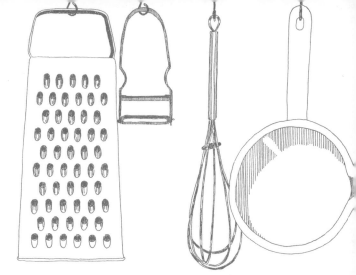

Essential Kitchen Equipment

In terms of equipment, some things are worth spending money on, because they will last for lengthy periods of time. Good-quality knives and decent pots and pans are most definitely worth investing in. I have a serious addiction to beautiful wooden chopping boards and, if recent studies are to be believed, they are actually the most hygienic boards to use in the kitchen, beating marble and plastic hands down.

So here's my list of essential kitchen equipment. It is fairly substantial, but think about how you want to cook, then go through the list and see what applies to you. I've included the basics but obviously the list will grow as you start cooking.

3 REALLY GOOD SHARP KNIVES (BIG, SMALL AND BREAD)

2 LIGHT WOODEN CHOPPING BOARDS

COLANDER (HANDY FOR DRAINING PASTA, WASHING VEGGIES, ETC.)

SALAD SPINNER

1 REALLY BIG SAUCEPAN OR POT

2 GREAT NON-STICK FRYING PANS

2 LARGE BAKING TRAYS

2 SPRING-FORM CAKE TINS

2 MUFFIN/CUPCAKE/BUN TRAYS

2 LOAF TINS

2 LARGE ROASTING TRAYS

SIEVE

LADLE

BOX GRATER

MICROPLANE GRATER

PEELER

CAN OPENER

POTATO MASHER

2 LARGE PYREX DISHES

MIXING BOWLS

WOODEN SPOONS

MEASURING SPOONS

WEIGHING SCALES

1 LARGE WHISK

1 SMALL WHISK

SPATULA

TONGS

MEALS IN MINUTES

Everyone's been there: you come in the front door after a long day and the last thing you want to do is start cooking. Well, here are some great options for quick dishes that, with a bit of forward planning, will have you fed in as little time as it takes to put your feet up. I'm know I'm repeating myself, but eating really well usually comes down to having a well-stocked store cupboard and a little preparation goes a very long way. You must know that feeling of peering hopelessly into an empty cupboard, searching desperately for a solution for dinner. What you need in those situations is some pre-marinated meat, which you already took out of the freezer that morning and left to defrost while you were at work, or else a big batch of pre-cooked rice or pasta, or even just some leftovers. All of these can be transformed into tasty dinners and can mean the difference between a good home-cooked meal or ending up with a Chinese takeaway! Getting excited about food and cooking will mean that you're way more likely to bother preparing great meals and hopefully you will find yourself thinking 'What's for dinner?' long before dinner time finally sneaks up on you.

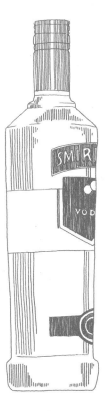

VODKA PENNE

For this recipe I need to thank the fantastic Lorraine Fanneran, who runs the equally fantastic and award-winning La Cucina in Limerick with her Italian husband, Bruno. She is an expert at delicious little pasta dishes and this one definitely proves that. Parents, don't worry: the alcohol burns off in the cooking, and anyway, the kids will be mightily impressed that you're giving them vodka. Lorraine suggests 4 tablespoons of vodka (plus a few in a glass for yourself depending on how bad your day has been!).

SERVES 4

350G (12OZ) PENNE

25G (1OZ) BUTTER

125G (4½OZ) PANCETTA OR BACON BITS, OR 2 SLICES COOKED HAM, CHOPPED

4 TBSP VODKA

200ML (7FL OZ) DOUBLE CREAM

3 TBSP TOMATO PURÉE

A SMALL HANDFUL OF FRESH FLAT LEAF PARSLEY, ROUGHLY CHOPPED

SEA SALT AND FRESHLY GROUND BLACK PEPPER

FRESHLY GRATED PARMESAN CHEESE, TO SERVE

- Cook the pasta in a large saucepan according to the instructions on the packet.

- Meanwhile, heat the butter in a large frying pan over a medium heat, add the pancetta and fry for 3–5 minutes until golden. Add the vodka and allow to simmer for a minute before adding the cream, tomato purée and parsley. Simmer gently for 5 minutes until the sauce has thickened. Season to taste with salt and black pepper.

- When the pasta is cooked, drain and add it to the sauce and mix through. Serve with a sprinkle of Parmesan cheese.

DIG-IN BEEF FAJITAS

If you're on the lookout for a rockin' little dinner dish to serve up to friends for a quick bite, these beef fajitas are going to blow you away. Sometimes I make twice the amount as they always go down so well.

SERVES 4

4 GARLIC CLOVES, PEELED AND FINELY CHOPPED

JUICE OF ½ LIME

1 TSP WORCESTERSHIRE SAUCE

2 TSP CHILLI POWDER

1 TSP DRIED OREGANO

1 TSP GROUND CUMIN

1 TSP FRESHLY GROUND BLACK PEPPER

400G (14OZ) STRIPLOIN STEAK, THINLY SLICED

2 TBSP SUNFLOWER OIL

2 RED ONIONS, PEELED AND THINLY SLICED

3 PEPPERS (RED, GREEN AND YELLOW), SLICED INTO STRIPS

A SMALL HANDFUL OF FRESH CORIANDER, ROUGHLY CHOPPED

SEA SALT

8 WHOLEMEAL TORTILLA WRAPS

TO SERVE

HOMEMADE GUACAMOLE (SEE PAGE 78)

SOURED CREAM

100G (3½OZ) CHEDDAR CHEESE, GRATED

- In a large bowl, combine the garlic, lime juice, Worcestershire sauce, chilli powder, oregano, cumin and black pepper then add the beef and toss until coated. Cover and place in the fridge.

- Heat half the sunflower oil in a large frying pan over a medium heat, add the onions and peppers and fry for 3–4 minutes until caramelised. Set the vegetables aside in a dish.

- Add the remaining oil to the pan and fry the marinated beef for 3 minutes until cooked but still tender. Make sure the pan is hot before cooking the beef. Add the reserved onions and peppers and the coriander and stir through then season with salt to taste.

- Heat the tortilla wraps in the microwave according to the packet instructions and cover with foil to keep warm.

- To assemble, spread a little guacamole on a tortilla, add some steak, peppers and onions and then top with soured cream and cheese. You may want to give a quick demo to your guests on how to do it, otherwise it may get messy.

Crispy Fish with a Warm Tangy Noodle Salad

When I'm cooking for people who don't love fish, I always find that if you funk things up a little and serve it differently to how they may have had it before, you can easily win them over. This tangy and crispy fish dish should do the trick.

SERVES 4

6 TBSP PLAIN FLOUR

1 TSP FRESHLY GROUND BLACK PEPPER

1 TSP SALT

½ TSP CHILLI POWDER

1 EGG

500G (1LB 2OZ) SKINLESS WHITE FISH FILLETS, SUCH AS HADDOCK OR COD, CUT INTO BITE-SIZED PIECES

SUNFLOWER OIL, FOR SHALLOW-FRYING

NOODLES

400G (14OZ) FLAT RICE NOODLES

1 TBSP SUNFLOWER OIL

3 GARLIC CLOVES, PEELED AND FINELY CHOPPED

1 THUMB-SIZED PIECE OF FRESH ROOT GINGER, PEELED AND FINELY CHOPPED

1 RED CHILLI, FINELY CHOPPED

6 SPRING ONIONS, FINELY SLICED ON DIAGONAL, PLUS EXTRA TO SERVE

1 TBSP SOY SAUCE

JUICE OF 1 LIME

- Cook the noodles according to the instructions on the packet. Drain and set aside.

- In a large wok or frying pan, heat the oil over a high heat, add the garlic, ginger and chilli and stir-fry for about 40-50 seconds until they are sizzling and aromatic. Add the spring onions and fry for a further minute. Pour in the soy sauce and lime juice, bring to a steady simmer and cook for 2 minutes.

- Take the pan off the heat and tumble in the cooked noodles, tossing to combine. Set aside and keep warm.

- For the fish, combine the flour with the pepper, salt and chilli powder on a large plate. Beat the egg in a bowl. Dip the fish first in the spicy flour, shaking off any excess, then dip in the beaten egg and then again in the spicy flour mix until coated then place on a plate and repeat with the remaining fish pieces.

- Pour enough oil into a large frying pan until it is about 1cm (½in) deep and heat over a high heat. Shallow-fry the fish pieces for 1-2 minutes on each side until golden. Remove with a slotted spoon and drain on a plate lined with kitchen paper.

- Serve the fish on top of the noodles with a few extra slices of spring onion.

CAJUN SPATCHCOCK CHICKEN

This combination of spices is so tasty, but if you don't have them all, don't be afraid to try dried or fresh herbs instead. The cooking time on a barbecue can be tricky to judge because it depends on the size of your chickens – if you are worried the meat isn't cooked, simply insert a skewer into the thickest part and if the juices run clear, the bird is ready. It's definitely best to leave the chickens to marinate for some time, but if you're in a rush, just cover with the paste and cook straightaway.

SERVES 6–8

2 SMALL CHICKENS
(1.1–1.4KG/2½–3LB EACH)

MARINADE

4 GARLIC CLOVES, PEELED

2 TBSP SOFT DARK BROWN SUGAR

2 TBSP PAPRIKA

2 TSP CAYENNE PEPPER

2 TSP DRIED OREGANO

A SMALL HANDFUL OF FRESH
SAGE LEAVES, ROUGHLY CHOPPED

A HANDFUL OF FRESH THYME SPRIGS

JUICE OF 1 LEMON

3–4 TBSP VEGETABLE OIL

A GENEROUS PINCH OF SEA
SALT AND FRESHLY GROUND
BLACK PEPPER

- To prepare each chicken, place the bird breast side down and, using a sharp knife or scissors, cut along either side of the back bone to remove it. Open the bird out, flip it breast side up and, using your fist, push down hard on the breast to break the bone. Thread a skewer diagonally through the bird from the leg to the breast and repeat on the other side. Using the sharp knife, score the bird on the legs and breasts then repeat the whole process for the second chicken. Place the chickens in a large roasting tray.

- Put all the ingredients for the marinade in a mortar or food processor and pound with a pestle or blitz in the machine until you have a rough paste. Spread the paste over the chickens until they are completely covered. Cover with foil and allow to marinate in the fridge for 30–60 minutes.

- Light a barbecue or preheat the oven to 200°C (400°F), Gas mark 6 if the weather is not up to cooking outdoors.

- Place the birds on the barbecue over a medium heat and cook breast side up for 25–30 minutes. Turn the birds over and cook for a further 15–20 minutes until the chickens are cooked through. If you find the meat is blackening too much, move to the edge of the barbecue or place the chickens on some foil until they are cooked through. Alternatively, oven roast the chickens for 50–60 minutes until cooked through.

CAJUN CHICKEN AND AVOCADO WRAPS

This little recipe makes a regular last-minute lunch for me.

SERVES 2

2 SKINLESS CHICKEN BREASTS, THINLY SLICED

1 TBSP CAJUN SEASONING

1 TBSP SUNFLOWER OIL

4 WHOLEMEAL TORTILLA WRAPS

2 TBSP CRÈME FRAÎCHE

A HANDFUL OF MIXED SALAD LEAVES

1 LARGE AVOCADO, PEELED, STONED AND CUT IN THICK SLICES

- Toss the chicken in the Cajun seasoning.

- Heat the oil in a large frying pan and fry the chicken for 3–4 minutes until tender, sizzling and cooked through. Remove from the pan and set aside.

- Assemble each wrap with a dollop of crème fraîche, some salad leaves, a few slices of avocado and a little Cajun chicken, then wrap, roll and ROCK!

STICKY MARMALADE ROAST CHICKEN DRUMSTICKS

This marinade also works well with duck or even a whole roasted chicken. Don't be afraid to experiment.

SERVES 4

2 TBSP MARMALADE

1 TBSP WHITE WINE VINEGAR

1 TBSP WHOLEGRAIN MUSTARD

1 TBSP OLIVE OIL

SEA SALT AND FRESHLY GROUND BLACK PEPPER

10 CHICKEN DRUMSTICKS, WITH SKIN ON

QUICK BULGUR WHEAT, TO SERVE (SEE PAGE 39)

- Preheat the oven to 200°C (400°F), Gas mark 6.

- Put the marmalade, vinegar, mustard, oil and a good pinch of salt and black pepper in a large roasting tray and whisk to combine. Add the chicken drumsticks to the tray and toss until the chicken is completely covered in the sauce.

- Roast in the oven for 40 minutes until the chicken drumsticks are cooked through, basting halfway through the cooking time.

- When cooked, remove the chicken from the oven and place on a plate with any leftover sticky juices spooned over. Serve with the bulgur wheat.

Simple Pasta Carbonara

My previous carbonara recipe had an ingredients list that included onions, garlic and crème fraîche. However, my eyes have now been opened. This recipe is so much closer to what a true Italian would cook, and the good news is that it's also much easier. It makes a really quick little supper.

SERVES 4

400G (14OZ) SPAGHETTI

1 TBSP OLIVE OIL

225G (8OZ) PANCETTA OR BACON BITS

50G (2OZ) PARMESAN CHEESE, GRATED

4 EGG YOLKS

SEA SALT AND FRESHLY GROUND BLACK PEPPER

- Cook the pasta in a large saucepan according to the instructions on the packet.

- Meanwhile, heat the olive oil in a large frying pan over a medium heat, add the pancetta and fry for 2–3 minutes until crisp. If the pancetta is quite fatty, you won't need the oil, as it will release its own fat.

- Drain the spaghetti, reserving a little of the cooking water. Return the pasta to the saucepan and, while it is still steaming hot, add the Parmesan cheese, egg yolks and cooked pancetta and season with salt and black pepper. Quickly stir everything together to give a creamy coating to the pasta.

- Serve straightaway, as the pasta can become a bit stodgy if left in the pan for too long. All the more reason to get it out of the pan and into your belly!

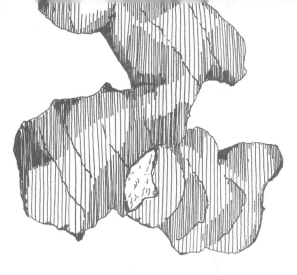

HEALTHY SINGAPORE NOODLES

Singapore noodles are a standard Chinese-restaurant dish, but making them at home is so easy. It also means you can monitor what's going into them, adding whatever healthy vegetables you feel like. The addition of curry powder not only brings a new flavour, but it also coats the noodles and gives a great texture to every bite.

SERVES 2

3 GARLIC CLOVES, PEELED AND FINELY CHOPPED

1 THUMB-SIZED PIECE OF FRESH ROOT GINGER, PEELED AND GRATED

2 TBSP SOY SAUCE

1 TBSP OYSTER SAUCE

2 SKINLESS CHICKEN BREASTS, SLICED INTO THIN STRIPS

100G (3½OZ) RICE VERMICELLI NOODLES

2 TBSP SUNFLOWER OIL

2 CELERY STICKS, FINELY SLICED

1 CARROT, PEELED AND FINELY SLICED

4 SPRING ONIONS, THINLY SLICED

1 TBSP ASIAN CURRY POWDER

A GOOD HANDFUL OF BEAN SPROUTS

1 TSP SESAME OIL, TO TASTE

- In a large, shallow non-metallic dish, combine the garlic, ginger, 1 tablespoon of soy sauce and the oyster sauce. Add the chicken and toss until coated, then cover and place in the fridge to marinate for at least 30 minutes.

- Soak the noodles in a bowl of boiling water for 6 minutes, or according to the packet instructions, until soft. Drain and set aside.

- Heat a wok or frying pan over a high heat, pour in the sunflower oil and swirl the pan to coat the sides. Add the chicken, including the marinade, and stir-fry for 3–4 minutes. Add the celery, carrot and spring onions and stir-fry for 2 minutes. Sprinkle in the curry powder and toss through for a further 2 minutes.

- Add the noodles, bean sprouts and sesame oil to the wok and, using kitchen tongs, toss everything together until well combined. Serve straightaway.

Chilli, Garlic and Lemon Mackerel

I have some amazing childhood memories of sunny, mackerel-filled summers with my grandad Do, out on his boat, my cousins and me racing to pull in the fishing rods with their heavy lines and a fish on each hook. My grandad would gut them and fillet them like the pro that he was, belly-laughing at the fact that we were all too squeamish to take them off the lines ourselves (and that still hasn't changed). For me, mackerel dishes should always be simple with really fresh flavours, so I love this quick and simple lunch which also has a great kick of heat thanks to the chilli.

SERVES 4

4 LARGE MACKEREL, GUTTED

OLIVE OIL, FOR DRIZZLING

2 LEMONS, CUT INTO SLICES

3 GARLIC CLOVES, PEELED AND FINELY CHOPPED

1 RED CHILLI, FINELY CHOPPED

SMOKED SEA SALT AND FRESHLY GROUND BLACK PEPPER

A SQUEEZE OF LEMON JUICE, TO SERVE

° Preheat the grill to high or light a barbecue.

° Place the mackerel on a plate, drizzle each one with olive oil inside and out then stuff with the lemon slices, garlic and chilli. Season with a good pinch of salt and black pepper.

° Cook the mackerel under the hot grill for 4–5 minutes on each side or place in a fish basket and cook on the barbecue for the same amount of time.

° Place the fish on a large serving dish, drizzle with a little extra olive oil and season with a generous squeeze of lemon juice. Serve straightaway.

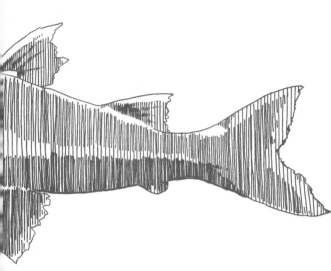

BAKED TERIYAKI SALMON

This is a perfect little dish for entertaining. I used to cook it in a frying pan, but came up with this much better method when I had a group of friends over for dinner and discovered that cooking the salmon in the oven makes it far easier to serve up in one piece. Make sure to use dark soy sauce here as it gives the salmon a great deep colour. It's definitely best to marinate the fish for some time, but if you're in a rush, just toss in the marinade and cook straightaway.

SERVES 6

2 TBSP DARK SOY SAUCE

1 TBSP CHINESE RICE WINE

1 TBSP HONEY

1 TBSP SOFT DARK BROWN SUGAR

JUICE OF 1 LIME

1 TSP SESAME OIL

1 LARGE RED CHILLI, FINELY CHOPPED

2 GARLIC CLOVES, PEELED AND MINCED

6 SKINLESS SALMON FILLETS

A HANDFUL OF SESAME SEEDS, TOASTED IN A DRY FRYING PAN (SEE PAGE 61)

6 SPRING ONIONS, THINLY SLICED

○ In a non-metallic high-sided dish, whisk the soy sauce, rice wine, honey, sugar, lime juice, sesame oil, chilli and garlic together until combined. Add the salmon and toss in the marinade to coat. Cover and place in the fridge for 1 hour (if you have time).

○ Preheat the oven to 200°C (400°F), Gas mark 6.

○ Arrange the salmon in a roasting tray and pour over the remaining marinade. Bake in the oven for 10–15 minutes until cooked through. Serve the salmon sprinkled with toasted sesame seeds and spring onions sprinkled on top.

ASIAN PORK AND VEGETABLE STIR-FRY

Pork loin normally comes in a long vacuum-pack and is great to pick up from the supermarket when it's on special offer and pop in the freezer until you need it. It's a really handy cut of meat as it's incredibly versatile and is quite easy to work with. Sometimes you may need to trim the fat off the sides, but don't worry too much about it if you are pushed for time.

SERVES 4

1 THUMB-SIZED PIECE OF FRESH ROOT GINGER, PEELED AND FINELY CHOPPED

1 RED CHILLI, DESEEDED AND FINELY CHOPPED

2 GARLIC CLOVES, PEELED AND FINELY CHOPPED

1 PORK LOIN FILLET (ABOUT 500G/ 1LB 2OZ), VERY THINLY SLICED

2 TBSP DARK SOY SAUCE

1 TBSP OYSTER SAUCE

1 TBSP HONEY

1 TSP FISH SAUCE (NAM PLA)

JUICE OF ½ LIME

2 CARROTS, PEELED AND FINELY SLICED

3 RED PEPPERS, FINELY SLICED

150G (5OZ) SUGAR SNAP PEAS, SLICED ON THE DIAGONAL

6 SPRING ONIONS, CUT INTO FAT SLICES ON THE DIAGONAL

1-2 TBSP SUNFLOWER OIL

FRESHLY COOKED RICE OR NOODLES, TO SERVE (OPTIONAL)

- Divide the ginger, chilli and garlic evenly between two bowls.

- Add the pork slices and 1 tablespoon of the soy sauce to the first bowl, tossing to combine.

- Add the oyster sauce, honey, fish sauce, lime juice and remaining soy sauce to the second bowl and whisk to combine. Add the carrots, peppers, sugar snap peas and spring onions, tossing in the dressing until thoroughly coated.

- Heat a little sunflower oil in a large wok or frying pan over a high heat, add the pork and the marinade and fry for 2-3 minutes until cooked through. Remove from the wok and set aside.

- You may want to add another drop of oil to the pan at this point. Add the dressed vegetables and fry for 3-4 minutes until tender but with still a bit of bite to them. When the veggies are ready, throw the pork back into the wok and toss to combine.

- Serve straightaway as it is or with some rice or noodles.

BAKED TRAY OF SHELLFISH WITH LEMON, CHILLI AND GARLIC

I created this simple but, let me tell you, highly impressive little dish for a romantic New Year's Eve dinner a few years back, and it went down a storm. It does of course help if your partner loves shellfish. If you haven't cooked shellfish before, don't be scared to have a go, as this dish is a great way to try it for the first time, alongside the more familiar flavours of garlic, chilli and lemon. You can use any shellfish you want, so feel free to experiment and don't panic if you can't get them all.

SERVES 2

250G (9OZ) LIVE MUSSELS (ABOUT A HANDFUL)

250G (9OZ) LIVE CLAMS (ABOUT A HANDFUL)

4 TBSP BUTTER, SOFTENED

6 TBSP OLIVE OIL

A FEW FRESH THYME SPRIGS

4 GARLIC CLOVES, PEELED AND FINELY CHOPPED

1 RED CHILLI, FINELY CHOPPED

6 CRAB CLAWS

4 SHELLED SCALLOPS

6 LARGE RAW PRAWNS, UNPEELED

SEA SALT

JUICE OF 1 LEMON, PLUS EXTRA TO SERVE

LEMON WEDGES, TO SERVE

CHOPPED FRESH FLAT-LEAF PARSLEY, TO SERVE

- Preheat the oven to 200°C (400°F), Gas mark 6.

- Place the mussels and clams in a sink filled with cold water and scrub away any dirt or beards. Discard any shells which are open at this point and which don't close when tapped on a hard surface.

- Place the butter, olive oil, thyme, garlic and chilli on a plate and mash together with the back of a fork.

- Arrange the shellfish on a large baking tray and coat with the butter mixture as well as you can. Sprinkle with a little salt and the lemon juice. Bake in the oven for 10 minutes until all the shellfish are cooked. Discard any shells that are still closed.

- Serve with an extra squeeze of lemon juice, lemon wedges and a sprinkle of fresh parsley.

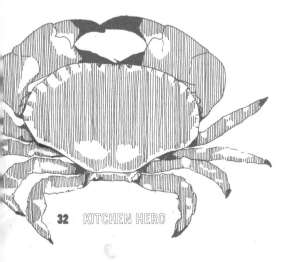

Stuffed Chicken Breasts with Balsamic Roast Peppers

This is one of my mum's specialities. She is the queen of the quick dinner and, despite working full time while we were kids, she always managed to have a hot tasty meal on the table in 30 minutes, come hell or high water. 'So you'd better bloody eat it!'

SERVES 4

110G (4OZ) FRESH WHITE BREADCRUMBS

50G (2OZ) READY-TO-USE SUN-DRIED TOMATOES, ROUGHLY CHOPPED

3 TBSP PESTO (SEE PAGE 155)

SEA SALT AND FRESHLY GROUND BLACK PEPPER

4 LARGE CHICKEN BREASTS, WITH SKIN AND ON THE BONE

2 LARGE RED PEPPERS, CUT INTO SLICES

1–2 TBSP BALSAMIC VINEGAR

3 TBSP OLIVE OIL

- Preheat the oven to 200°C (400°F), Gas mark 6.

- Combine the breadcrumbs, sun-dried tomatoes and pesto in a bowl then season with a generous amount of salt and black pepper.

- Arrange the chicken breasts in a roasting tray and, using a sharp knife, make a slit lengthways along the side of each breast, but don't cut the whole way through. Stuff the inside of the chicken pocket with a heaped tablespoon of the stuffing mix.

- Toss the pepper slices in a little balsamic vinegar and half the olive oil and arrange around the chicken breasts. Finally drizzle the chicken with the remaining olive oil and season with salt and black pepper.

- Roast in the oven for 20–30 minutes until the chicken is golden and cooked through. Serve with a few of the caramelised pepper slices on top.

HERBY SPAGHETTI AMATRICIANA

Pasta is a great store-cupboard ingredient that can easily be transformed into a super little supper. This is a really easy recipe, packed with flavour from the delicious ingredients.

SERVES 4

300G (11OZ) SPAGHETTI

2 TBSP OLIVE OIL

1 ONION, PEELED AND FINELY CHOPPED

2 GARLIC CLOVES, PEELED AND FINELY CHOPPED

250G (9OZ) PANCETTA OR BACON BITS

1 TSP DRIED CHILLI FLAKES

2 X 400G TINS CHOPPED TOMATOES

SEA SALT AND FRESHLY GROUND BLACK PEPPER

A HANDFUL OF FRESH FLAT LEAF PARSLEY, ROUGHLY CHOPPED

A HANDFUL OF FRESH BASIL, ROUGHLY CHOPPED

A SMALL HANDFUL OF FRESHLY GRATED PARMESAN CHEESE, TO SERVE

- Cook the pasta in a large saucepan according to the instructions on the packet.

- Meanwhile, heat the olive oil in another large saucepan over a medium heat, add the onion and garlic and fry slowly until soft. Add the pancetta and chilli flakes and fry until crisp. Stir in the chopped tomatoes. Bring to the boil then reduce the heat and cook at a gentle simmer for 15 minutes until the sauce has reduced by half. Season with a good pinch of salt and black pepper and stir through the parsley and basil.

- When the pasta is cooked, drain and add it to the spicy tomato sauce. Toss until the pasta is coated. Serve straightaway with a little grated Parmesan.

OATS AND SEEDS CRUSTED FISH WITH LEMON

This is a great twist on homemade fish fingers and is a super way to pack even more nutrients into kids' dinners without them even realising.

SERVES 4

3 TBSP WHOLEMEAL FLOUR

SEA SALT AND FRESHLY GROUND BLACK PEPPER

3 TBSP ROLLED OATS

3 TBSP MIXED SEEDS

1 LARGE EGG

4 SKINLESS WHITE FISH FILLETS, SUCH AS HADDOCK OR COD (150–200G/5–7OZ EACH), SLICED INTO ROUGH CHUNKS

SUNFLOWER OIL, FOR SHALLOW-FRYING

TO SERVE

MIXED LEAF SALAD

LEMON WEDGES

- Combine the flour and a generous amount of salt and black pepper on one plate and the oats and seeds on another. Beat the egg in a shallow dish.

- Dip a piece of fish first in the flour, shaking off any excess, then dip in the beaten egg and lastly in the oats and seeds mix. Place on a plate and repeat with the rest of the fish.

- Pour enough oil into a large frying pan until it is about 1cm (½in) deep and heat over a high heat. Fry the fish for 2–3 minutes on each side until golden brown. Remove with a fish slice and drain on a plate lined with kitchen paper

- Serve with a mixed leaf salad and wedges of lemon.

QUICK AND SIMPLE BEEF IN BLACK BEAN SAUCE

A fairly classic dish, but you can really pump up the flavours when making it at home. It takes just minutes to prepare and gives you delicious results.

SERVES 4

400G (14OZ) WHOLEWHEAT NOODLES

400G (14OZ) RUMP STEAK, THINLY SLICED

1 LARGE THUMB-SIZED PIECE OF FRESH ROOT GINGER, PEELED AND CRUSHED

3 GARLIC CLOVES, PEELED AND CRUSHED

1 RED CHILLI, FINELY CHOPPED

5-6 SPRING ONIONS, THINLY SLICED

3 TBSP SESAME OIL

SUNFLOWER OIL, FOR FRYING

1 TSP SOFT DARK BROWN SUGAR

1 TBSP CHINESE RICE WINE

3 TBSP DARK SOY SAUCE

5 TBSP BLACK BEAN SAUCE

JUICE OF 1 LIME

A GOOD HANDFUL OF FRESH CORIANDER, ROUGHLY CHOPPED

- Cook the noodles according to the instructions on the packet, drain and set aside.

- In a bowl, combine the beef, ginger, garlic, chilli and spring onions with the sesame oil.

- Heat a large wok or frying pan over a high heat, add a little sunflower oil and swirl to coat the sides. Add the beef mixture and stir-fry for 3–4 minutes until the beef is tender. Add the sugar, rice wine, soy sauce and black bean sauce and stir to combine. Cook for a further minute and add the lime juice.

- Transfer the beef mixture to a large serving dish, leaving a little of the sauce in the wok. Throw the cooked noodles and the coriander into the wok and toss together. Serve the noodles and beef in the same dish and bring to the table.

Prosciutto, Mozzarella and Sage Pork Chops with Quick Bulgur Wheat

This is one of my super-speedy suppers which can easily be thrown together the minute you come in the door. Bulgur wheat is my little superhero store-cupboard ingredient. It's a wheat grain that has already been cooked, dried and cracked so it has a short cooking time. It is like a very nutty couscous, doesn't take long to prepare and is packed with health benefits. It's also cheap as chips.

SERVES 4

4 LARGE PORK CHOPS

FRESHLY GROUND BLACK PEPPER

4 LARGE FRESH SAGE LEAVES

110G (4OZ) MOZZARELLA CHEESE, CUT INTO 4 THIN SLICES

4 SLICES OF PROSCIUTTO (ABOUT 60G/2½OZ)

BULGUR WHEAT

250G (9OZ) BULGUR WHEAT

1 TSP VEGETABLE BOUILLON POWDER

250G (9OZ) CHERRY TOMATOES, ROUGHLY CHOPPED

A GOOD HANDFUL OF FRESH BASIL, ROUGHLY CHOPPED

DRIZZLE OF EXTRA VIRGIN OLIVE OIL

SEA SALT

- Put the bulgur wheat in a bowl with the vegetable bouillon powder. Cover with about twice the volume of boiling water and stir to combine. Cover with cling film and set aside for 10–15 minutes until the bulgur wheat has soaked up all the water.

- Preheat the grill to medium-high.

- Place the pork chops on a plate and season both sides with black pepper. Press a large sage leaf onto one side of each chop then turn over and place a slice of mozzarella on the other side. Now comes the opportunity to show off your *Blue Peter* skills by wrapping each pork chop in prosciutto. My best advice is to lay a slice of prosciutto on a flat board, place a chop on top, sage side down, and then simply wrap the slice around the chop.

- Arrange the chops on a grill tray and cook under the hot grill for 3–4 minutes on each side until cooked through.

- When the bulgur wheat is cooked, stir through, then drain off any excess water. Add the tomatoes, basil and olive oil and season with salt.

- Serve the pork chops with a generous portion of bulgur wheat and feel happy that you served up a tasty dinner in a matter of minutes.

CREAMY SPINACH CHICKEN PASTA

I love recipes that come with a dash of nostalgia and this one never fails to deliver. In what now feels like another life, I was in a band with my Swedish pal Jonathan and, while staying at his place, I picked up this great recipe from his 'Mama', Kerstin. She really knows how to feed a crowd and this dish is absolutely delicious.

SERVES 4

300G (11OZ) TAGLIATELLE

A KNOB OF BUTTER

400G (14OZ) SKINLESS CHICKEN BREASTS, SLICED INTO THICK STRIPS

3 GARLIC CLOVES, PEELED AND FINELY CHOPPED

50G (2OZ) READY-TO-USE SUN-DRIED TOMATOES

150G (5OZ) BABY SPINACH LEAVES

250ML (8½FL OZ) SINGLE CREAM

A GENEROUS PINCH OF SEA SALT AND FRESHLY GROUND BLACK PEPPER

- Cook the pasta according to the instructions on the packet.

- Meanwhile, heat the butter in a large frying pan over a high heat and, when foaming, fry the chicken for 4–6 minutes until cooked through. Add the garlic, sun-dried tomatoes and spinach and fry until the spinach has wilted.

- Add the cream, bring to a steady simmer and cook for 3–4 minutes, then season with salt and black pepper. Once the pasta is cooked, drain and add to the sauce. Toss well and serve straightaway.

Omelette with Tomato and Avocado

This is great as a snack or a quick-fix breakfast. I picked up the recipe during a stay in the fast-paced city of LA. We ate it in a great little café, right before my uncle (and wannabe surf instructor) Niall, who lives there, dragged us out to Santa Monica beach for a surfing lesson.

SERVES 1
VEGETARIAN

2 LARGE EGGS

A DROP OF MILK

**SEA SALT AND FRESHLY GROUND
BLACK PEPPER**

1 TBSP BUTTER

**½ AVOCADO, STONED, PEELED AND
CUT INTO CHUNKY SLICES**

**6 CHERRY TOMATOES,
SLICED IN QUARTERS**

- Whisk the eggs and milk in a bowl until combined. Season with a pinch of salt and black pepper.

- Heat a small frying pan, about 20cm (8in) in diameter, over a high heat and add the butter to the pan. When it is foaming, pour in the eggs and, using a spatula, pull the edges of the omelette towards the centre so that the beaten egg runs to the outside. Continue doing this for 1–2 minutes until there is no runny egg left.

- While the omelette is still a little soft on top, fold it towards the centre and then hold the pan over the plate and nudge it off and onto the plate. Be careful not to overcook the omelette – it will continue to set as you dish it up.

- Serve topped with the avocado slices and quartered cherry tomatoes, plus an extra grinding of salt and black pepper.

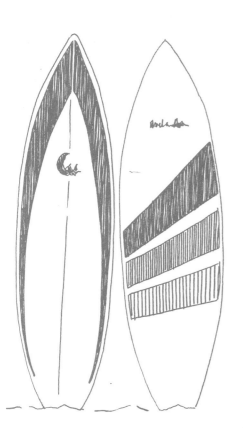

'BOOM BOOM POW' NASI GORENG

The first question I always get asked when I mention this dish is 'What the hell is nasi goreng?', so first things first, let me explain it for you. It's basically fried rice that's been kicked up the arse, sent on a rocket around the moon and back with a good whack of chilli and a fried egg on top just in case you weren't awake! It sounds a little complicated but really it's just a case of prepping the paste, slicing the meat and cooking the eggs. The rice is better if cooked and cooled well in advance (even the day before). I promise if you try this once, you will definitely make it again.

SERVES 4

2 TBSP GROUNDNUT OIL

4 GARLIC CLOVES, PEELED

2 RED CHILLIES, PLUS 1 SLICED RED CHILLI TO SERVE

1 TSP CORIANDER SEEDS

1 TBSP FISH SAUCE (NAM PLA)

1 TBSP TOMATO KETCHUP

2 LARGE SHALLOTS, PEELED AND ROUGHLY CHOPPED

3 TBSP SUNFLOWER OIL

300G (11OZ) RAW KING PRAWNS, PEELED AND DEVEINED

2 SKINLESS CHICKEN BREASTS, FINELY SLICED

250G (9OZ) BASMATI RICE, COOKED AND COOLED

1 TBSP DARK SOY SAUCE

1 TBSP KECAP MANIS (INDONESIAN SWEET SOY SAUCE)

2 SPRING ONIONS, SLICED, PLUS EXTRA TO SERVE

4 LARGE EGGS

PRAWN CRACKERS, TO SERVE (OPTIONAL)

- Blitz the groundnut oil, garlic, chillies, coriander seeds, fish sauce, tomato ketchup and shallots in a food processor until you have a smooth paste.

- In a large wok or deep frying pan, heat 1 tablespoon of the sunflower oil over a high heat. Add a spoonful of the paste and stir-fry for 1 minute until you get all those amazing aromas going! Add the prawns and chicken and stir-fry for a further 2–3 minutes until just cooked through. Set aside and keep warm.

- Using another tablespoon of the oil, fry the remaining paste as before and then add the cooked rice, soy sauce, kecap manis and spring onions and fry for 3–4 minutes until the rice is coated and piping hot. Return the chicken and prawns to the wok and toss well until hot.

- Divide the nasi goreng among four plates and quickly fry the eggs in the remaining oil in a frying pan.

- Serve each plateful topped with a fried egg, a sprinkle of sliced spring onions and chilli, and some prawn crackers if you want.

ASIAN PORK LETTUCE CUPS

I want to introduce you to what is easily one of my favourite little dinner-party treats. This dish tastes amazing and I hope it will become one of your staple entertaining recipes. The meat mix is full of really light and aromatic flavours and is served in baby gem lettuce leaves, making it perfect finger food.

SERVES 4

1 TBSP SUNFLOWER OIL

250G (9OZ) LEAN PORK MINCE

3 GARLIC CLOVES, PEELED AND FINELY CHOPPED

1 RED CHILLI, DESEEDED AND FINELY CHOPPED

1 TBSP FISH SAUCE (NAM PLA)

1 TBSP DARK SOY SAUCE

1 TBSP CASTER SUGAR

5 SPRING ONIONS, FINELY CHOPPED

8 FRESH MINT LEAVES, FINELY CHOPPED

JUICE OF 1 LIME

TO SERVE

2 BABY GEM LETTUCES, SEPARATED INTO LEAVES

THAI SWEET CHILLI SAUCE

- Heat the sunflower oil in a large frying pan over a high heat, add the pork mince and fry for 2–3 minutes until the mince is tender, breaking the meat up with a wooden spoon as it cooks. Add the garlic and chilli and fry for a further minute.

- Add the fish sauce, soy sauce and sugar and stir through, frying for another minute until you have a good colour on the meat. Finally add half the spring onions and mint and all the lime juice and fry for 1–2 minutes until the spring onions are just tender. Remove from the heat and allow to cool until just warm.

- Place 1 heaped tablespoon of the aromatic pork in each baby gem lettuce leaf, top with a drizzle of Thai sweet chilli sauce and garnish with the remaining spring onions and mint.

PARTY FOOD & DRINKS

As much as I enjoy a really good, hearty, home-cooked meal, sometimes I take more pleasure in picking at small mouthfuls that are packed with intense flavours. So while all of the recipes in this chapter are perfect for parties, I also have to admit that I love some of them as a sneaky dinner, eaten just by me when I'm all alone. Party food is a chance to sample lots of different flavours and tastes all at once, and an opportunity to experiment with fresh ideas, so I try to think outside of the box. Like any home cook, I find the desire to impress always sneaks its way into my thought process if I'm cooking a meal for other people. Preparation is definitely the key to success and will avoid you having too much to cook when your guests finally arrive. My method is to always have the main bulk of things prepared in advance, so that when people come through the door it's just a case of assembly. Getting your guests involved in the actual cooking is another way to take the pressure off: I've had some great parties where everyone has made their own pizza, assembled their own fajitas or even rolled their own sushi! Perhaps get guests involved with mixing cocktails – these can be really fun to make and will definitely get the party started. I have included recipes for some of my favourite ones, as well as a few recipes for mocktails, which are non-alcoholic, so great for kids and very refreshing on hot summer days.

ROAST AUBERGINE DIP AND CRISPY HERB AND GARLIC PITTAS

This dip makes a fantastic addition to what my best buddy Jonathan refers to as 'The Spread'. Which, roughly translated, is the collection of snacks you churn out for guests to dig into at a party.

SERVES 4
VEGETARIAN

2 AUBERGINES

3 GARLIC CLOVES, PEELED AND FINELY CHOPPED

JUICE OF ½ LEMON

2 TBSP EXTRA VIRGIN OLIVE OIL, PLUS EXTRA FOR DRIZZLING

SEA SALT AND FRESHLY GROUND BLACK PEPPER

2 TBSP NATURAL YOGHURT

2 TBSP CHOPPED FRESH CORIANDER, PLUS EXTRA TO SERVE

CRISPY HERB AND GARLIC PITTAS

3 GARLIC CLOVES, PEELED AND FINELY CHOPPED

2 TSP DRIED OREGANO

4 TBSP OLIVE OIL

6 WHOLEMEAL PITTA BREADS, SLICED INTO ROUGH CHUNKS

A GOOD PINCH OF SEA SALT AND GROUND BLACK PEPPER

° Preheat the oven to 200°C (400°F), Gas mark 6.

° Pierce the aubergines all over with a fork and place on a baking tray. Roast in the oven for 40 minutes until tender.

° Remove the aubergines from the oven and allow to cool slightly before scraping the flesh from the skin and transferring it to a bowl. Add the garlic, lemon juice and extra virgin olive oil and mix through. Season to taste with salt and black pepper. Finally stir in the yoghurt and chopped coriander.

° To make the crispy herb and garlic pittas, whisk the garlic, oregano and olive oil together in a bowl. Dip the pitta slices into the mixture to coat them, then place on a baking tray and bake in the oven for about 12 minutes until crisp.

° Serve the dip with an extra drizzle of olive oil and sprinkle of coriander on top and the crispy baked pittas on the side.

Spicy Buffalo Chicken Wings

I remember being very confused as a kid as to how buffaloes could have wings but, as I'm sure you know, they are in fact chicken wings. Something you might *not* know is that the name 'Buffalo wings' actually comes from their place of origin, Buffalo NY, in the USA. But the story that buffaloes might have the ability to fly will still always go down well with any younger guests! These spicy wings are damn tasty and should be served with some crisp celery to cool your mouth down.

SERVES 6–8

110G (4OZ) BUTTER

120ML (4½FL OZ) HOT PEPPER SAUCE (LOUISIANA)

½ TBSP WORCESTERSHIRE SAUCE

½ TSP PAPRIKA

½ TSP CAYENNE PEPPER

SEA SALT AND FRESHLY GROUND BLACK PEPPER

1.3KG (3LB) CHICKEN WINGS

CELERY STICKS, TO SERVE

BLUE CHEESE DIP

100ML (4FL OZ) SOURED CREAM

110G (4OZ) BLUE CHEESE, CRUMBLED

120ML (4½FL OZ) MAYONNAISE

½ TBSP LEMON JUICE

3 GARLIC CLOVES, PEELED AND FINELY CHOPPED

- Preheat the oven to 200°C (400°F), Gas mark 6.

- Whisk the butter, hot pepper sauce, Worcestershire sauce, paprika, cayenne pepper and salt and black pepper together in a saucepan over a high heat. Bring to the boil then reduce the heat and simmer for 10 minutes until slightly thickened.

- Arrange the chicken wings on two large roasting trays and pour over half the sauce. Toss to coat and bake in the oven for 40 minutes until cooked through. Place the wings in a large bowl. Reheat the remaining sauce and pour over the wings, then toss lightly until coated.

- Blitz the ingredients for the blue cheese dip in a food processor until smooth and creamy. Serve with the warm wings and a handful of celery sticks.

Mini Caramelised Onion and Goat's Cheese Tarts

I am pretty much addicted to these flavours, all wrapped up in deliciously crumbly pastry, and perfect for bite-size nibbles!

**SERVES 6,
MAKES 12 MINI TARTS**

A GOOD KNOB OF BUTTER

1 TBSP OLIVE OIL

2 ONIONS, PEELED, HALVED
  AND SLICED INTO HALF MOONS

1 TBSP BALSAMIC VINEGAR

1 TBSP SOFT DARK BROWN SUGAR

SEA SALT AND FRESHLY
  GROUND BLACK PEPPER

450G (1LB) FROZEN PUFF PASTRY
  (2 SHEETS)

PLAIN FLOUR, FOR DUSTING

1 LARGE EGG, BEATEN

6 TBSP PESTO (SEE PAGE 155)

A GOOD HANDFUL OF FRESH BASIL,
  ROUGHLY CHOPPED

110G (4OZ) GOAT'S CHEESE,
  CUT INTO 12 PIECES

EQUIPMENT

A 6CM (2½IN) PASTRY CUTTER

- Heat the butter and olive oil in a frying pan over a high heat, add the onions and fry for 7–8 minutes until golden. Add the balsamic vinegar and sugar, then season with salt and black pepper, reduce the heat and cook gently until you have a thick gloopy onion mixture. Remove the pan from the heat and allow to cool.

- Unroll the pastry sheets and, using the pastry cutter, press out 12 circles.

- Dust a baking tray with a little flour and arrange the puff pastry circles on the tray. Prick the centre of each circle 3–4 times with a fork and brush the edges with a little egg.

- Spoon a little pesto into the centre of each circle, then top with some basil, a piece of goat's cheese and a little of the caramelised onions.

- Bake in the oven for 10–15 minutes until the pastry has puffed up and is golden.

PARMESAN AND POPPY SEED PUFF PASTRY STRAWS

When entertaining, sometimes I skip a starter and instead have a selection of little bites that people can nibble on before the main event. These puff pastry straws sound complicated but they take literally a few moments to prepare and leave you with something very impressive to serve to your guests.

**SERVES 6-8,
MAKES ABOUT 24 STRAWS**

PLAIN FLOUR, FOR DUSTING

450G (1LB) FROZEN PUFF PASTRY (2 SHEETS)

1 EGG, BEATEN

50G (2OZ) PARMESAN CHEESE, GRATED

1-2 TBSP POPPY SEEDS

SEA SALT AND FRESHLY GROUND BLACK PEPPER

○ Preheat the oven to 200°C (400°F), Gas mark 6. Sprinkle two baking trays with a tablespoon of flour.

○ Unroll the first pastry sheet on a floured work surface. Brush with some beaten egg and sprinkle with half the Parmesan cheese and poppy seeds. Season with salt and black pepper. Gently press the topping into the pastry and cut into about twelve 2.5cm (1in) strips. Twist each strip twice in one direction and lay it on a prepared baking tray. Do the same with the second sheet of pastry.

○ Bake in the oven for 8-10 minutes until golden and the pastry has puffed up. Allow to cool before serving.

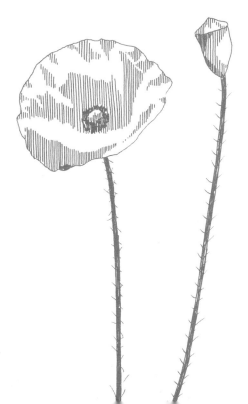

Tesse's Cheesy Tortilla Chips

I always keep a few simple entertaining dishes up my sleeve to impress with minimum effort. Such as these tasty baked tortilla chips, an idea I got from my lovely friend Tesse. They are made in a matter of minutes and are perfect with drinks. I normally use Cheddar, but feel free to experiment with different types of cheese. Sometimes I also add sliced red onion to give the chips an extra hit of flavour.

SERVES 4-6
VEGETARIAN

1 X 200G BAG OF PLAIN TORTILLA CHIPS

1 X 235G JAR OF TOMATO SALSA

150G (5OZ) CHEDDAR CHEESE, GRATED

- Preheat the oven to 200°C (400°F), Gas mark 6.

- Place the tortilla chips on a large baking sheet. Spoon half a teaspoon of salsa onto each chip and top with a little grated cheese.

- Bake in the oven for 6–8 minutes until the cheese goes a lovely golden brown. Serve straightaway.

GARLIC-RUBBED CIABATTA TOAST

This is my no-fuss version of garlic bread. Don't bother using loads of butter and chopping the garlic; just toast some really good-quality chewy ciabatta with a crispy crust, rub with a clove of garlic, drizzle with olive oil and season with some flaky sea salt.

SERVES 4-6
VEGETARIAN

1 LARGE CIABATTA LOAF (ABOUT 250G/9OZ)

OLIVE OIL, FOR DRIZZLING

2 LARGE GARLIC CLOVES, PEELED AND CUT IN HALF

SEA SALT FLAKES

- Preheat the grill to medium.

- Slice the ciabatta into 1cm ($\frac{1}{2}$in) slices and drizzle with olive oil on both sides. Arrange on a grill tray and place under the hot grill to toast on both sides.

- Rub one side of each piece of toast with the cut garlic cloves and season with some sea salt. Serve straightaway.

PULLED-PORK BURGERS

Although these are not exactly normal burgers, this recipe is a must-try! They are another American invention and make the best of an offcut of pork, resulting in delicious, mouth-wateringly tender meat doused in a sticky, spicy sauce.

SERVES 6–8

1 BONELESS PORK SHOULDER (ABOUT 1.5KG/3LB 5OZ)

6–8 BURGER BUNS, HALVED

RED CABBAGE AND CARROT COLESLAW (SEE PAGE 110)

MARINADE

1 LARGE ONION, PEELED AND FINELY CHOPPED

6 GARLIC CLOVES, PEELED AND ROUGHLY CHOPPED

2 TSP CHILLI POWDER

1 TSP CORIANDER SEEDS

2 TBSP DRIED ENGLISH MUSTARD

175ML (6FL OZ) DISTILLED WHITE VINEGAR

1 TSP PAPRIKA

5 TBSP TOMATO KETCHUP

2 TSP WORCESTERSHIRE SAUCE

1 TBSP TREACLE

50G (2OZ) SOFT DARK BROWN SUGAR

1 TSP SALT

- Blitz all the ingredients for the marinade in a blender or using a pestle and mortar until you have a smooth mixture.

- Place the pork in a large saucepan or flameproof casserole dish, add the marinade and turn the pork in it until coated. Cover and place in the fridge to marinate for a couple of hours, or overnight if you have time. If you don't have time, don't worry; just cook the meat.

- Place the pan or casserole dish over a high heat, add about 1 litre (1$\frac{3}{4}$ pints) water, just enough to cover the meat, and bring to the boil. Reduce the heat, cover with a lid and cook at a steady simmer for about 1$\frac{1}{2}$ hours until the meat pulls apart easily with a fork. (The cooking time depends on the cut of meat, so you may have to cook it for a longer period of time until you end up with really tender pork.) Make sure to turn the pork during cooking.

- Remove the pork from the sauce with a carving fork and shred, then place the shredded meat on a warm plate, cover with foil and set aside. Bring the sauce to a steady simmer and reduce for 8–10 minutes until it is thick.

- Lightly toast the burger bun halves, if you wish, then spoon the sauce over the pork and serve in the toasted buns with a little coleslaw.

SEARED BEEF CROSTINI WITH ROCKET, PARMESAN AND PINE NUTS

These seared beef crostini are perfect finger food for hungry guests and never fail to impress. You may want to double the recipe as they always go down really well. Toast the pine nuts in a dry frying pan over a high heat; they crisp up really quickly so keep an eye on them and make sure they don't burn.

MAKES 8 MINI BEEF CROSTINI

110G (4OZ) SIRLOIN OR STRIPLOIN STEAK

SEA SALT AND FRESHLY GROUND BLACK PEPPER

SUNFLOWER OIL, FOR FRYING

50G (2OZ) ROCKET LEAVES

50G (2OZ) PINE NUTS, LIGHTLY TOASTED

A GOOD HANDFUL OF PARMESAN CHEESE SHAVINGS

8 SLICES OF GARLIC-RUBBED CIABATTA TOAST (SEE PAGE 57)

EXTRA VIRGIN OLIVE OIL, FOR DRIZZLING

DRESSING

3 TBSP EXTRA VIRGIN OLIVE OIL

1 TBSP BALSAMIC VINEGAR

1 GARLIC CLOVE, PEELED AND CRUSHED

A GOOD PINCH OF SEA SALT AND FRESHLY GROUND BLACK PEPPER

- Season the steak with a good grinding of black pepper on both sides.

- Heat a drop of sunflower oil in a frying pan over a high heat, add the steak and cook for 2–3 minutes on each side for medium-rare. Transfer the steak to a plate, cover with foil and allow to rest while you prepare the dressing.

- Whisk all the ingredients for the dressing together in a large bowl. Add the rocket and toasted pine nuts and toss to combine.

- Slice the steak thinly, season with salt and toss in the juices that have run off.

- Assemble the crostini by placing a couple of slices of beef on each ciabatta slice. Add a couple of rocket leaves and a scattering of toasted pine nuts, then top with shavings of Parmesan, a final grinding of black pepper and a drizzle of olive oil.

Zingy Thai Fishcakes

Fishcakes really are so simple to make. You basically bung all the ingredients in a food processor, shape the fish cakes and then fry them. It couldn't be easier. Experiment with the flavours – I like my fish cakes spicy so I add a chilli to kick up the heat, but you can leave it out if you prefer.

SERVES 4

450G (1LB) SKINLESS WHITE FISH FILLETS, SUCH AS HADDOCK OR COD

1 TBSP FISH SAUCE (NAM PLA)

1 LARGE EGG

A GOOD HANDFUL OF FRESH CORIANDER, ROUGHLY CHOPPED, PLUS EXTRA TO SERVE

1 TBSP RED CURRY PASTE

1 RED CHILLI (OPTIONAL), PLUS AN EXTRA ONE, SLICED TO SERVE

2 GARLIC CLOVES, PEELED

1 THUMB-SIZED PIECE OF FRESH ROOT GINGER, PEELED AND FINELY CHOPPED

FINELY GRATED ZEST AND JUICE OF 1 LIME, PLUS LIME WEDGES TO SERVE

75G (3OZ) GREEN BEANS, FINELY SLICED

5-6 SPRING ONIONS, ROUGHLY CHOPPED

4 TBSP VEGETABLE OIL

THAI SWEET CHILLI SAUCE, TO SERVE

- Place the fish in a food processor and blitz for 3 seconds or so until smooth. Add the fish sauce, egg, coriander, curry paste, chilli, garlic, ginger and lime zest and juice and blitz again until everything is combined. Remove the blade from the food processor and stir through the green beans and just over half the spring onions.

- With damp hands, form the mixture into 12 balls and flatten to make fish cakes.

- Heat the oil in a large frying pan over a high heat and fry the fishcakes in two batches for about 2 minutes on each side. Remove with a fish slice and drain on a plate lined with kitchen paper.

- Garnish with the remaining spring onions, a few slices of chilli (if using) and some chopped coriander. Serve straightaway with lime wedges and Thai sweet chilli sauce.

RED ONION AND AVOCADO LAMB BURGERS

I absolutely love lamb burgers because the flavours always remind me of summer. When you get the weather, these are great on the barbie. If you can't get your hands on lamb mince, you can, of course, replace it with minced pork or beef.

SERVES 4

500G (1LB 2OZ) LAMB MINCE

1 TBSP OLIVE OIL

1 ONION, PEELED AND FINELY CHOPPED

3 GARLIC CLOVES, PEELED AND FINELY CHOPPED

1 TSP DRIED OREGANO

½ TSP SALT

½ TSP FRESHLY GROUND BLACK PEPPER

½ TSP GROUND CUMIN

1 TBSP TOMATO KETCHUP

1 TSP WORCESTERSHIRE SAUCE

TO SERVE

4 LARGE BURGER BUNS, HALVED

2 AVOCADOS, PEELED, STONED AND ROUGHLY SLICED

1 RED ONION, PEELED AND FINELY SLICED

A GOOD HANDFUL OF ROCKET LEAVES

○ Preheat the grill to medium.

○ Combine all the ingredients for the burgers in a large bowl. Using your hands, divide the mixture into four portions and form into palm-sized burgers.

○ Arrange the burgers on a grill tray and place under the hot grill to cook for 4–5 minutes on each side.

○ Serve each burger in a bun with slices of avocado and red onion and a few rocket leaves.

CHICKEN TERIYAKI BURGERS

Chicken burgers are always a nice change from the regular beefburger, and marinating them in this teriyaki mix will really kick things up a notch. Do try and marinate them for as long as you can; if you want, you could place the chicken breasts and the marinade in a zip-lock bag and leave in the freezer for up to three months, ready to rock whenever you need them.

SERVES 4

4 SKINLESS, BONELESS CHICKEN BREASTS

4 GARLIC CLOVES, PEELED AND CRUSHED

4 TBSP TERIYAKI SAUCE

1 TBSP HONEY

JUICE OF ½ LIME

SUNFLOWER OIL, FOR BRUSHING

TO SERVE

4 SESAME BURGER BUNS, HALVED

5-6 SPRING ONIONS, FINELY CHOPPED ON THE DIAGONAL

MAYONNAISE (SEE PAGE 173)

- Place the chicken breasts in a large shallow bowl with the garlic, teriyaki sauce, honey and lime juice and mix until the breasts are coated. Cover and place in the fridge to marinate for at least an hour or overnight if you have the time.

- Heat a large griddle pan or non-stick frying pan over a high heat and brush with a little sunflower oil. Place the marinated chicken breasts in the pan and cook for 3–4 minutes on each side until cooked through and golden brown.

- Toast the burger buns on both sides, then serve each chicken breast in a toasted bun with some spring onions and a good dollop of mayonnaise.

COCKTAIL MEATBALLS

This is adapted from my Auntie Annie's recipe, which she picked up while living in America. You might think it's strange that the recipe calls for tinned soup, but bear with me – it works. After everything has finished bubbling away, you will be left with the most amazing meatballs, which are inexcusably sweet and moreish and will have your guests returning for seconds and thirds. It is a great dish to make in advance and pull out of the fridge to reheat when you are ready. Serve on the most kitsch and retro cocktail sticks you can get your hands on.

SERVES 8

450G (1LB) BEEF MINCE

½ LARGE ONION, PEELED AND FINELY CHOPPED

½ GREEN PEPPER, FINELY CHOPPED

4 TBSP FRESH WHITE BREADCRUMBS

1 LARGE EGG, BEATEN

A DASH OF TABASCO SAUCE

½ TSP SALT

SAUCE

30G (1¼OZ) BUTTER

½ LARGE ONION, PEELED AND FINELY CHOPPED

½ GREEN PEPPER, FINELY CHOPPED

1 X 340G TIN CONDENSED TOMATO SOUP

2 TBSP SOFT DARK BROWN SUGAR

1 TBSP WHITE WINE VINEGAR

1 TBSP WORCESTERSHIRE SAUCE

1 TSP ENGLISH MUSTARD

- Preheat the grill to high.

- In a large bowl, combine the minced beef, onion, green pepper, breadcrumbs, egg and Tabasco sauce until thoroughly mixed together.

- Form the mixture into bite-sized meatballs each about 3cm (1¼in) in diameter. Arrange the meatballs on a grill tray and place under the hot grill for 10–12 minutes, turning from time to time, until browned all over.

- To make the sauce, melt the butter in a saucepan over a medium-high heat, add the onion and pepper and sauté until soft. Add the remaining ingredients and bring to the boil, then reduce the heat and simmer gently for 5 minutes.

- Arrange the meatballs on a serving platter and cover with the sauce, then pass around and enjoy!

BACON-WRAPPED BLT BEEF BURGERS

The BLT is one of my favourite sandwiches, so when I saw burgers wrapped in bacon during a trip to America, I had a brainwave. The BLT burger was born!

SERVES 4

500G (1LB 2OZ) BEEF MINCE

2 GARLIC CLOVES, PEELED AND FINELY CHOPPED

1 TBSP TOMATO KETCHUP

1 TSP DIJON MUSTARD

SEA SALT AND FRESHLY GROUND BLACK PEPPER

8 SLICES OF STREAKY BACON

TO SERVE

4-6 BURGER BUNS, HALVED

MAYONNAISE (SEE PAGE 173)

1 LARGE VINE OR BEEF TOMATO, CUT INTO CHUNKY SLICES

2 HEADS OF BABY GEM LETTUCE, FINELY SLICED

4 TSP DIJON MUSTARD (OPTIONAL)

○ Preheat the grill to medium.

○ In a large bowl, combine the minced beef, garlic, tomato ketchup, mustard and a generous pinch of salt and black pepper. Form the mixture into 4–6 burgers and wrap each burger with two slices of bacon.

○ Arrange the burgers on a grill tray and place under the hot grill to cook for 4–5 minutes on each side.

○ Toast the burger bun halves on both sides then serve each burger in a bun with a good dollop of mayonnaise, a slice or two of tomato and some sliced lettuce. If you want an extra kick, add a teaspoonful of mustard.

Chorizo and Spring Onion Quesadillas

You can get chorizo either in soft, thin slices or in thick sausage form. I use the sausage variety for this recipe. If you are really stuck and can't get your hands on any chorizo, don't panic; you can use a little leftover cooked chicken or some sliced cooked ham as a substitute. The great thing about quesadillas is that you can adapt them to use whatever you have: the classic ones just need some tomato salsa, cheese and thinly sliced red onion – simple and delicious!

SERVES 2

150G (5OZ) CHORIZO, SLICED INTO BITE-SIZED CHUNKY ROUNDS

1 GARLIC CLOVE, PEELED AND CRUSHED

A SMALL HANDFUL OF CHERRY TOMATOES (ABOUT 150G/5OZ), FINELY CHOPPED

SEA SALT AND FRESHLY GROUND BLACK PEPPER

4 WHOLEMEAL TORTILLA WRAPS

75G (3OZ) CHEDDAR CHEESE, GRATED

5 SPRING ONIONS, FINELY SLICED, PLUS EXTRA TO SERVE

- Heat a large non-stick frying pan over a high heat and cook the chorizo on both sides until sizzling and roaring red. Remove the chorizo from the pan and place on a plate lined with kitchen paper. Drain a little of the chorizo oil from the frying pan, leaving enough to fry the quesadillas.

- While the chorizo is frying, combine the garlic and chopped tomatoes in a bowl and season with a little salt and black pepper.

- Spread half the tomato and garlic mix on one of the tortilla wraps, top with a little grated cheese, a generous amount of spring onions and just under half of the cooked chorizo. Place another tortilla wrap on top and press it down gently. Carefully place the quesadilla in the frying pan and fry for 2 minutes on each side over a high heat, until the quesadilla is golden brown and the cheese inside has melted. Repeat with the second quesadilla.

- Slice the quesadillas into quarters and serve them with an extra sprinkle of sliced spring onions and chorizo.

STICKY BARBECUE SPARE RIBS

I have to admit to being a bit addicted to these ribs, mainly because this recipe makes them exactly how I like them, full of finger-lickin' flavour and falling-off-the-bone tenderness. The trick is to simmer them gently until the meat is tender. The recipe makes enough for six, but I have been known to eat them all by myself sat in the corner of the kitchen in a sticky mess!

SERVES 6

3KG (6½LB) BABY BACK PORK RIBS

2 ONIONS, PEELED AND SLICED IN HALF

1 BULB OF GARLIC, UNPEELED AND TOP SLICED OFF

A GENEROUS PINCH OF SEA SALT

BARBECUE SAUCE

60G (2½OZ) DEMERARA SUGAR

4 TBSP DARK SOY SAUCE

4 TBSP TOMATO KETCHUP

4 TBSP HONEY

4 GARLIC CLOVES, PEELED AND FINELY CHOPPED

1 TBSP DRIED ENGLISH MUSTARD

2 TSP TABASCO SAUCE

- Cut the strips of ribs into manageable pieces, with about 3-4 ribs to each piece, then put the ribs in a large saucepan with the onions, garlic, a generous pinch of salt and enough cold water to cover. Bring to the boil then reduce the heat and simmer gently for 1-1½ hours until the meat is tender.

- Shortly before the ribs are cooked, preheat the grill to medium or light a barbecue.

- Whisk all the ingredients for the barbecue sauce together in a saucepan. Bring to the boil over a high heat, then reduce the heat and simmer for about 5 minutes until you have a thick sauce.

- Remove the ribs from the pan and place in a large baking dish or roasting tray, then coat with half the barbecue sauce. Cook under the hot grill or on the barbecue for 5 minutes on each side and then serve with the rest of the barbecue sauce (reheated if necessary) and devour!

INDIVIDUAL BROCCOLI QUICHES

These quiches are mini ones, which makes them super easy to serve and perfect for picnics or nibbles. You don't need miniature tins – just use a bun tray.

SERVES 6
VEGETARIAN

225G (8OZ) PLAIN FLOUR, PLUS EXTRA FOR DUSTING

A PINCH OF SALT

125G (4½OZ) COLD BUTTER, CUT INTO SMALL PIECES

FILLING

1 HEAD OF BROCCOLI, BROKEN INTO SMALL FLORETS

3 LARGE EGGS

300ML (10½FL OZ) DOUBLE CREAM

SEA SALT AND FRESHLY GROUND BLACK PEPPER

150G (5OZ) MATURE CHEDDAR CHEESE, GRATED

EQUIPMENT

A 6-HOLE BUN TRAY

AN 8.5CM (3½IN) DIAMETER PASTRY CUTTER OR GLASS

- To make the pastry, place the flour and salt in a large bowl. Add the butter and, using your fingertips, rub it into the flour until the mixture resembles rough breadcrumbs. Sprinkle over 1–2 tablespoons of water and bring the dough together to form a ball. Wrap in cling film and place in the fridge to rest for at least 10 minutes.

- For the filling, first blanch the broccoli in a pan of boiling water for 1 minute, then drain and cool under cold running water. Drain well and put on a plate lined with kitchen paper to absorb any extra water while you work with the pastry.

- Preheat the oven to 180°C (350°F), Gas mark 4 and place a baking tray on the middle shelf.

- Roll out the pastry on a lightly floured work surface and cut out six circles using the pastry cutter or glass. Place the circles in the hollows of the bun tray. Prick the bases with a fork and place in the oven for about 10 minutes until lightly golden. Remove and set aside.

- Whisk the eggs and cream together in a bowl. Season with salt and black pepper and add the broccoli and cheese. Divide the filling between the mini pastry cases and return to the oven for 30–35 minutes until the filling is set and golden on top.

RUSTIC STEAK SANDWICHES

These are proper Saturday afternoon sandwiches. The right bread makes all the difference – some chewy, crispy ciabatta is perfect here. If you don't fancy making your own aïoli, you can cheat by smashing a garlic clove with the back of a knife until you have a smooth paste and then mix it with a little store-bought mayonnaise.

SERVES 2

2 X 125G (4OZ) STRIPLOIN OR RIB EYE BEEF STEAKS

SEA SALT AND FRESHLY GROUND BLACK PEPPER

1 TBSP SUNFLOWER OIL

2 CIABATTA ROLLS, CUT IN HALF

HOMEMADE AÏOLI (SEE PAGE 173)

25G (1OZ) ROCKET LEAVES

½ RED ONION, PEELED AND FINELY SLICED

- Season the steaks generously with freshly ground black pepper.

- Heat the oil in a large frying pan over a high heat and fry the steaks for 2–3 minutes on each side for medium-rare. Transfer the steaks to a plate, cover with foil and allow them to rest for 5 minutes.

- Once the steaks have rested, slice them thinly, toss in the juices that have run off and season with salt. Toast the ciabatta halves on both sides

- Assemble the sandwiches by spreading the aïoli on two of the toasted ciabatta halves, adding the juicy steak slices, rocket and red onion, and topping with the remaining ciabatta halves. Enjoy!

SLOW-ROASTED CHERRY TOMATOES

Roasting brings out the flavour of any tomato, so even if they are out of season, this method will always come up with the goods.

SERVES 4
VEGETARIAN

3 TBSP OLIVE OIL

1 TBSP BALSAMIC VINEGAR

1 LARGE PUNNET OF CHERRY TOMATOES (ABOUT 500G/1LB 2OZ), SLICED IN HALF

SEA SALT AND FRESHLY GROUND BLACK PEPPER

- Preheat the oven to 190°C (375°F), Gas mark 5

- In a bowl, whisk together the olive oil and balsamic vinegar. Add the tomatoes and toss to combine.

- Arrange the tomatoes cut side up on a large baking tray and season with a good pinch of salt and black pepper. Roast in the oven for about 45 minutes until the tomatoes have reduced in size and are slightly charred. Allow to cool then eat warm or at room temperature.

ROAST SWEET POTATO CUBES WITH ROSEMARY

It's little sides like these that really make a meal. I sometimes use these beautiful sweet-potato cubes instead of croûtons in salads. You can also make them with normal potatoes.

SERVES 4
VEGETARIAN

3-4 SWEET POTATOES, PEELED AND CUT INTO SMALL CUBES

3 LARGE FRESH ROSEMARY SPRIGS

1 TBSP OLIVE OIL

SEA SALT AND FRESHLY GROUND BLACK PEPPER

- Preheat the oven to 200°C (400°F), Gas mark 6.

- Place the sweet potato cubes in a roasting tray with the rosemary sprigs and drizzle with the olive oil. Toss together until all the cubes are coated. Season generously with salt and black pepper.

- Place in the oven to roast for 35-40 minutes until the cubes are crispy on the outside and soft in the centre. Serve immediately.

Homemade Guacamole

Guacamole is extremely adaptable and all about personal taste. Some recipes call for tomatoes, lemon juice or parsley but I like mine with a kick so I add a drop of Tabasco sauce for some heat. Avocados need a generous seasoning of salt to bring out their great natural flavour.

SERVES 4–6
VEGETARIAN

2 RIPE AVOCADOS

2 GARLIC CLOVES, PEELED AND FINELY CHOPPED

2 TBSP EXTRA VIRGIN OLIVE OIL

JUICE OF ½ LIME, PLUS LIME WEDGES TO SERVE

1–2 DASHES OF TABASCO SAUCE

½ RED ONION, PEELED AND FINELY CHOPPED

A SMALL HANDFUL OF FRESH CORIANDER, ROUGHLY CHOPPED, PLUS EXTRA TO GARNISH

SEA SALT AND FRESHLY GROUND BLACK PEPPER

- Slice each avocado in half, remove the stone then spoon out the flesh into a bowl. Add the garlic, olive oil, lime juice and Tabasco and mash with the back of a fork. You could also do your mashing using a pestle and mortar if you wish.

- When you have a rough mash, add the finely chopped onion and stir through the chopped coriander. Season well with salt and black pepper. Garnish with coriander and lime wedges and serve within an hour of making.

SWEET POTATO CRISPS

If you've ever been sucked in by one of those adverts about the wonders of a fancy kitchen slicing machine, now is the time to dig it out. A mandolin is a very handy tool, but it is not an everyday piece of equipment so generally gets shoved to the back of the cupboard. However, if you do have one, it makes easy work of finely slicing vegetables into thin crisps. If you don't have one, just do your best to slice them by hand using a sharp knife. The flavour of these crisps is so addictive. I suggest you make a massive batch because you're bound to be left wanting more.

SERVES 8
VEGETARIAN

4 SWEET POTATOES, UNPEELED AND FINELY SLICED

SUNFLOWER OIL, FOR COATING

SEA SALT AND FRESHLY GROUND BLACK PEPPER

- Preheat the oven to 200°C (400°F), Gas mark 6.

- Arrange the sliced sweet potatoes on two large baking sheets. Brush both sides with oil to coat and then sprinkle generously with salt and black pepper. Bake in the oven for 45 minutes until crisp.

Cocktails

Nothing gets a dinner party started more impressively than a good cocktail. They can be mostly prepared in advance, leaving just a light assembly job when you are ready to serve. If you can lay your hands on some cocktail umbrellas or other glitzy cocktail paraphernalia, these recipes will give you good reason to use them. It takes a brave man to sip a pink cocktail with an umbrella, but you might as well go the whole hog!

APPLE MARTINI

This is a stirred cocktail, as opposed to others which are blitzed with ice. It's really simple and really strong! I was introduced to it on a night out with my pals Jenny-Lee and Brian, and it has been the drink of choice any time we've caught up since.

SERVES 1

60ML (2½FL OZ) APPLE SCHNAPPS

30ML (1¼FL OZ) VODKA

30ML (1¼FL OZ) APPLE JUICE

1 CRISP GREEN APPLE SLICE,
  TO SERVE

- Pour the apple schnapps, vodka and apple juice into a jug or cocktail shaker filled with ice cubes. Stir well and strain into a chilled cocktail glass.

- Serve with a slice of crisp green apple.

MUDSLIDE

This was our favourite cocktail when I was on holiday in France with my pals Paulie, Shambo and PJ. I can only handle one or two – they're delicious but heavy-going! If you can, serve in big sundae glasses with over-the-top straws, umbrellas or wild cocktail decorations.

SERVES 4

100ML (4FL OZ) VODKA

100ML (4FL OZ) KAHLÚA COFFEE LIQUEUR

100ML (4FL OZ) BAILEYS IRISH CREAM

200ML (7FL OZ) SINGLE CREAM

200ML (7FL OZ) MILK

2 BANANAS, PEELED

TO SERVE (OPTIONAL)

WHIPPED CREAM

GRATED CHOCOLATE

- Place all the ingredients for the cocktail and a good handful of ice cubes in a food processor and blitz until smooth.

- Pour into glasses and serve with a topping of whipped cream and a sprinkle of grated chocolate if you're feeling wild!

STRAWBERRY DAIQUIRI

Now, although a strawberry daiquiri may not be the most manly of cocktails, it is my drink of choice and this is my recipe for foolproof, super-tasty daiquiris. I should add that this recipe does come with a warning – once you learn it, you may find yourself making them all too often! I use frozen strawberries as it is so convenient to have a few packets of them stocked up in the freezer and you end up with a really delicious slush. You can also substitute other frozen berries, so experiment with the ingredients.

SERVES 6

1 TBSP CASTER SUGAR,
  PLUS EXTRA FOR FROSTING (OPTIONAL)

1 LEMON OR LIME

400G (14OZ) FROZEN STRAWBERRIES

300ML (10$\frac{1}{2}$FL OZ) PRESSED APPLE JUICE

300ML (10$\frac{1}{2}$FL OZ) WHITE RUM

- To frost the glasses, put 2–3 tablespoons of caster sugar on a small plate. Cut a wedge of lemon or lime and use it to rub around the top edge of each glass. Turn the glasses upside down and dip in the sugar.

- Place the strawberries and a small handful of ice cubes in a food processor, then pour in the apple juice and rum and sprinkle in the sugar. Blitz for about 30 seconds until you get a smooth slushy mixture. Taste a teaspoonful, as you may need to add a little more sugar.

- Serve in the frosted glasses; it's the best way to enjoy them!

MOJITO

To really get the party started at a barbecue or summer get-together, I love bringing out a big mojito pitcher. People panic a little bit about the measurements for cocktails, but it really is a case of making them to taste and remembering simple rules like one part alcohol to three parts mixer for each person. Then just add the flavours! Get your hands on some fresh summer mint for these babies – it's one of the easiest herbs to grow, so just pick up a plant in the garden centre and pop it in a pot for fresh mint all summer long!

SERVES 4

4–5 FRESH MINT SPRIGS, PLUS EXTRA

60G (2$\frac{1}{2}$OZ) CASTER SUGAR

500ML (18FL OZ) SODA WATER

300ML (10$\frac{1}{2}$FL OZ) WHITE RUM

JUICE OF 3 LIMES, PLUS 2 LIMES CUT
  INTO WEDGES

- In a large pitcher or jug, mash the mint and sugar roughly together with a wooden spoon or the end of a rolling pin.

- Fill the pitcher with ice cubes and add the remaining ingredients. Stir, pour into glasses and garnish with mint sprigs.

FLAVOURED WATERS

While you're wowing your guests with stunning party food, it's always good to add that extra touch by serving nice big pitchers of interesting flavoured drinks. These are ideal when there are kids around, but even if you only have adult guests, it's still better to give people a non-alcoholic option.

Pink Lemonade

SERVES 8

JUICE OF 10 LEMONS

325G (12OZ) CASTER SUGAR

300ML (10$\frac{1}{2}$FL OZ) CRANBERRY JUICE

900ML (1 PINT 12FL OZ) SPARKLING WATER

A FEW TINNED PITTED CHERRIES,
  TO SERVE

- Stir the lemon juice and sugar in a large pitcher or jug until the sugar has dissolved. Pour in the cranberry juice, sparkling water and some crushed ice. Stir to combine and add the pitted cherries to serve.

Sparkling Ginger Pineapple Fizz

SERVES 8

200G (7OZ) CASTER SUGAR

100G (3$\frac{1}{2}$OZ) FRESH ROOT GINGER,
  PEELED AND FINELY CHOPPED

750ML (1 PINT 6FL OZ) PINEAPPLE JUICE

JUICE OF 3 LIMES

500ML (18FL OZ) SPARKLING WATER

- In a saucepan, slowly bring the sugar, 250ml (8$\frac{1}{2}$fl oz) of water and the ginger to the boil, stirring until the sugar has completely dissolved. Reduce the heat and simmer for 5 minutes until the liquid reduces and becomes a syrup. Set aside to cool.

- Strain the cooled syrup through a sieve into a large pitcher or jug and discard the ginger pieces. Pour in the pineapple juice, lime juice and sparkling water and add a little crushed ice. Stir to combine and serve straightaway.

Strawberry and Mint Iced Tea

SERVES 8-10

8 REGULAR TEA BAGS

4 FRESH MINT SPRIGS

250G (9OZ) CASTER SUGAR

500G (1LB 2OZ) STRAWBERRIES, HULLED AND HALVED

LEMON SLICES, TO SERVE

- In a large saucepan, bring 1 litre (1¾ pints) of water to the boil over a high heat. Remove from the hob and stir in the tea bags and mint. Cover and allow to steep for 5 minutes then strain and set aside to cool.

- In another saucepan, dissolve the sugar in 1 litre (1¾ pints) of water over a high heat, stirring occasionally until the sugar has dissolved. Set aside to cool.

- Place the strawberries in a large pitcher or jug and pour over the cooled mint tea and sugary water. Top with crushed ice, stir to combine and serve straightaway.

Mint and Lemon Iced Green Tea

SERVES 8-10

8 REGULAR TEA BAGS

10 FRESH MINT SPRIGS (20G PACKET), PLUS EXTRA TO SERVE

200G (7OZ) CASTER SUGAR

250ML (8½FL OZ) LEMON JUICE (JUICE OF ABOUT 5 LEMONS)

- In a large saucepan, bring 1 litre (1¾ pints) of water to the boil over a high heat. Remove from the hob and stir in the tea bags and mint. Cover and allow to steep for 5 minutes then strain and set aside to cool.

- In a large pitcher or jug, stir the sugar and lemon juice together until the sugar dissolves. Add some crushed ice and pour in 1 litre (1¾ pints) of water and the cooled tea.

- Serve with a few extra sprigs of fresh mint.

SALADS & SIDES

This is technically two chapters rolled into one, because although many of these recipes make the perfect accompaniment to any tasty main dish, they are also good enough to stand alone. I will often devour a big hearty salad or delicious side dish on its own and it will keep me more than satisfied. Remember that salads don't always have to be salads in the traditional sense. You can mix things up with fresh and punchy salsa salads, Asian-inspired salads of thinly sliced raw veggies, or great seasonal roast vegetable salads, particularly delicious in the winter. The recipes that make people go 'Wow!' are generally the simple ones, especially when they've been given a twist. I love creating a new take on a classic, such as giving sides an extra hit of herbs or spices, or serving them up in cool little personal portions. I have one bugbear about homemade salads, however: those pre-packed plastic bags of lettuce, which, although convenient, can be expensive and sometimes filled with nasty chemicals and gases. Preparing my own salad leaves is one the best kitchen habits I've picked up. Break the leaves off any head of lettuce and throw them into cold water, swill them around to let any dirt sink to the bottom, then leave in the water for a few minutes to crisp up before taking them out to dry. A salad spinner is ideal because it dries the leaves quickly – quite important, as moisture causes them to wilt. When the leaves are dry, wrap them in kitchen paper or a clean tea towel and place in the vegetable drawer of your fridge where they will stay fresh for 3–4 days.

GRIDDLED SPICY FISH WITH TOMATO SALSA SALAD

This is a fish salad that packs a punch. Fish can have quite a delicate flavour and is often best when it's cooked very simply, but sometimes I like to mix things up and pair it with really out-there flavours, such as this refreshing tomato salsa.

SERVES 4

2 TSP SWEET PAPRIKA

½ TSP GROUND CUMIN

½ TSP CAYENNE PEPPER

4 TUNA, SALMON OR SWORDFISH STEAKS (ABOUT 150G/5OZ EACH)

1 TBSP OLIVE OIL

TOMATO SALSA

4-6 TOMATOES, FINELY CHOPPED

2 RED PEPPERS, FINELY CHOPPED

2 SPRING ONIONS, FINELY CHOPPED

1 GARLIC CLOVE, PEELED AND FINELY CHOPPED

A SMALL HANDFUL OF FRESH CORIANDER, FINELY CHOPPED

JUICE OF 1 LIME

1 TBSP EXTRA VIRGIN OLIVE OIL

A GENEROUS PINCH OF SEA SALT AND FRESHLY GROUND BLACK PEPPER

- Place the paprika, cumin and cayenne pepper on a plate and then press the fish in the spice mix on both sides until nicely coated all over. Set aside while you make the salsa.

- Prepare the salsa by combining all the ingredients together in a bowl and tossing to combine.

- Brush the oil onto a large griddle pan or non-stick frying pan, set over a high heat and fry the fish steaks for 1–2 minutes on each side.

- Serve the fish with the salsa and tuck in!

CHICKEN SALAD WITH CHILLI, GINGER AND LIME DRESSING

My pal Michele loves this salad and when we used to travel together, I'd always have to make one for her otherwise she'd eat mine! Packed with tasty ingredients, this recipe is perfect for entertaining. You can prepare all the elements separately, stick them in the fridge and assemble the salad when your guests arrive. Don't be afraid to add other vegetables. Peppers, cucumber, spring onions and bean sprouts are all good additions.

SERVES 4

4 SKINLESS CHICKEN BREASTS (ABOUT 700G/1½LB), SLICED THINLY INTO STRIPS

1 CHINESE CABBAGE, THINLY SLICED

3 MEDIUM CARROTS, PEELED AND SLICED

1 RED ONION, PEELED AND THINLY SLICED

100G (3½OZ) SUGAR SNAP PEAS, SLICED

1 TBSP SUNFLOWER OIL

100G (3½OZ) CHOPPED PEANUTS

A HANDFUL OF CHOPPED FRESH CORIANDER

MARINADE

2 TBSP SOY SAUCE

JUICE OF ½ LIME

1 GARLIC CLOVE, PEELED AND CRUSHED

½ RED CHILLI, FINELY CHOPPED

½ THUMB-SIZED PIECE OF FRESH ROOT GINGER, PEELED AND FINELY CHOPPED

DRESSING

3 TBSP SUNFLOWER OIL

1 TBSP SOY SAUCE

1 TBSP SMOOTH PEANUT BUTTER

JUICE OF ½ LIME

1 TBSP HONEY

1 TSP SESAME OIL

1 GARLIC CLOVE, PEELED AND CRUSHED

½ RED CHILLI, FINELY CHOPPED

½ THUMB-SIZED PIECE OF FRESH ROOT GINGER, PEELED AND FINELY CHOPPED

- Mix all the marinade ingredients together in a bowl, add the chicken strips and mix through. Cover and place in the fridge to marinate while you prepare the salad and dressing.

- In a small bowl, whisk all the ingredients for the dressing together until combined.

- Place the Chinese cabbage, carrots, red onion and sugar snap peas in a large salad bowl. Add half the dressing and combine until all the vegetables are well coated.

- Heat the sunflower oil in a frying pan. Remove the chicken strips from the marinade and fry for 2–3 minutes on each side until golden brown and cooked through.

- Serve the salad in individual bowls topped with the chicken, a sprinkle of chopped peanuts, a little chopped coriander and an extra drizzle of the dressing.

INDIVIDUAL POTATO DAUPHINOISE

I mastered this classic dish a long time ago, so it's one I always like to play with. This is my latest version. By making it in individual portions, there is no hassle of dishing it up when it lands on the table. Instead, each guest gets their own little dish to munch their way through.
You can use a mandolin to slice the potatoes thinly, but if you don't have one, just slice them as thinly as possible with a sharp knife.

SERVES 4

300ML (10½FL OZ) MILK

300ML (10½FL OZ) DOUBLE CREAM

A PINCH OF FRESHLY GROUND NUTMEG

2 FRESH THYME SPRIGS

1 GARLIC CLOVE, PEELED AND SLICED

SEA SALT AND FRESHLY
  GROUND BLACK PEPPER

500G (1LB 2OZ) FLOURY POTATOES,
  PEELED AND THINLY SLICED

75G (3OZ) CHEDDAR CHEESE, GRATED

25G (1OZ) PARMESAN CHEESE, GRATED

EQUIPMENT

4 RAMEKINS OR SMALL
  OVENPROOF DISHES

∘ Preheat the oven to 200°C (400°F), Gas mark 6.

∘ Bring the milk, cream, nutmeg, thyme and garlic to a steady simmer in a saucepan and simmer for 5 minutes. Remove from the heat, season with salt and black pepper and set aside.

∘ Layer the potatoes in the ramekins or serving dishes, pressing them down to make them snug and tight, then pour the milk and cream mixture over each dish. Mix together the Cheddar and Parmesan cheese and sprinkle over the top, then place the ramekins on a baking tray.

∘ Bake in the oven for 40 minutes until golden on top and tender on the inside. Allow to stand for about 10 minutes before serving.

Wholegrain Mustard Roast Potatoes

Good roast potatoes are the staple of most families' Sunday roasts and many people have their own take on them. I add a little wholegrain mustard to mine for a bit of an edge.

SERVES 4
VEGETARIAN

3 TBSP WHOLEGRAIN MUSTARD

1 TBSP OLIVE OIL

3 GARLIC CLOVES, PEELED
AND FINELY CHOPPED

500G (1LB 2OZ) BABY POTATOES

SEA SALT AND FRESHLY
GROUND BLACK PEPPER

- Preheat the oven to 200°C (400°F), Gas mark 6.

- In a large bowl, whisk the wholegrain mustard, olive oil and garlic together until combined. Tumble the potatoes into the bowl and toss until they are coated.

- Arrange the potatoes in a roasting tray and season with salt and black pepper. Roast in the oven for about 40 minutes until crispy on the outside and tender on the inside. Serve straightaway as a delicious side dish.

Roast Pumpkin with Spinach, Walnut, Feta and Balsamic Dressing

If you don't have the time to roast the pumpkin, you can also make this salad with grilled Portobello mushrooms. Simply drizzle them with olive oil and place under a hot grill for a few minutes. Great flavours in no time at all!

SERVES 4
VEGETARIAN

900G (2LB) BUTTERNUT SQUASH OR PUMPKIN, PEELED, DESEEDED AND CUT INTO SLICES

3 TBSP EXTRA VIRGIN OLIVE OIL, PLUS EXTRA FOR DRIZZLING

SEA SALT AND FRESHLY GROUND BLACK PEPPER

1 TSP HONEY

1 GARLIC CLOVE, PEELED AND FINELY CHOPPED

1 TBSP BALSAMIC VINEGAR

75G (3OZ) BABY SPINACH LEAVES

100G (3½OZ) FETA CHEESE, CRUMBLED

2 HANDFULS OF WALNUTS, LIGHTLY TOASTED (SEE PAGE 102)

- Preheat the oven to 220°C (425°F), Gas mark 7.

- Place the butternut squash slices on a roasting tray, drizzle with a little olive oil and season with salt and black pepper. Roast in the oven for 40 minutes until they are nice and golden and slightly charred at the edges. Remove from the oven and allow to cool slightly on the tray while you prepare the rest of the salad.

- Whisk the honey, garlic, olive oil and balsamic vinegar together in a large bowl until combined. Add the spinach and toss to coat.

- Arrange the pumpkin slices on a large serving platter, add the dressed spinach then crumble over the feta and sprinkle with toasted walnuts.

Sweet and Spicy Carrot, Cabbage and Bean Sprout Salad

Something that can be quite frustrating about salads is that they often don't keep for very long; this means they are not always an ideal option for lunch boxes. This recipe is my lunch-box salad solution. The chunky, crunchy vegetables in this salad will happily sit coated in the dressing for 1–2 days. It doesn't taste half bad either, if I do say so myself. If you have a food processor with a vegetable slicing attachment hiding in your cupboard, now is the time to pull it out.

SERVES 4–6
VEGETARIAN

½ CHINESE CABBAGE, FINELY SLICED

150G (5OZ) BEAN SPROUTS

2 LARGE CARROTS, PEELED AND COARSELY GRATED

3-4 SPRING ONIONS, FINELY SLICED LENGTHWAYS

A HANDFUL OF BLACK OR WHITE SESAME SEEDS, TOASTED (SEE PAGE 61)

A HANDFUL OF CHOPPED FRESH CORIANDER (OPTIONAL)

DRESSING

1 TBSP CHINESE RICE WINE

1 TBSP SOY SAUCE

1 TBSP CASTER SUGAR

1 TSP TOASTED SESAME OIL

- In a large bowl, whisk together all the ingredients for the dressing until combined.

- Add the Chinese cabbage, bean sprouts, carrots and spring onions and toss to combine.

- Serve with a sprinkling of toasted sesame seeds and some chopped coriander if you like.

Sofie's Squashed Potatoes

Searching for your new favourite potato recipe? Well look no further, this might be it! Fluffy and full of flavour, with crispy skins, these little babies have it all. They were actually a result of my girlfriend Sofie dropping a pot of boiled potatoes all over the floor on her way to putting them in the roasting tray. After the screaming had died down, we creatively came up with these.

SERVES 4
VEGETARIAN

16 BABY POTATOES
(ABOUT 850G/1LB 13OZ)

2 GARLIC CLOVES, PEELED
AND FINELY CHOPPED

A FEW FRESH THYME SPRIGS

A FEW FRESH ROSEMARY SPRIGS,
FINELY CHOPPED

1 TSP DIJON MUSTARD

JUICE OF ½ LEMON

4 TBSP OLIVE OIL, PLUS EXTRA
FOR DRIZZLING

SEA SALT AND FRESHLY
GROUND BLACK PEPPER

- Preheat the oven to 200°C (400°F), Gas mark 6.

- Place the potatoes in a saucepan of cold water and bring to the boil over a high heat. Reduce the heat and simmer gently for 20 minutes until tender when pierced with a fork. Drain and set aside.

- Using a pestle and mortar or hand-held blender, blitz the garlic, herbs, mustard, lemon juice and olive oil together.

- Put the potatoes on a large baking tray, drizzle with a little olive oil and shake the tray to combine. Arrange the potatoes in rows on the baking tray and, using a potato masher, press down gently on each one until they are crushed on top. Spoon a little of the garlic herb mix onto each potato and season generously with salt and black pepper. Bake in the oven for 30 minutes until golden and crisp then serve immediately.

Sliced Waldorf Salad

Waldorf salad is a fairly established dish in the salad world, but my quick take on it is a little more elegant. By slicing the apple and celery as thinly as possible, I think the texture becomes far more interesting. I also make the dressing a little thinner so that it doesn't cling to the salad ingredients. I often make this alongside a few other salads for people to choose from at barbecues or home buffets.

SERVES 4
VEGETARIAN

50G (2OZ) WALNUTS

3 CELERY STICKS, THINLY SLICED ON THE DIAGONAL

2 CRISP GREEN APPLES, CORED AND THINLY SLICED

DRESSING

1 TBSP LEMON JUICE

3 TBSP MAYONNAISE

1 TBSP NATURAL YOGHURT

A GOOD PINCH OF SEA SALT AND FRESHLY GROUND BLACK PEPPER

○ Toast the walnuts in a dry frying pan over a medium heat for 2–3 minutes. Be careful as they burn easily. Remove the pan from the heat and set aside to cool.

○ In a large bowl, whisk the ingredients for the dressing together until combined. Add the walnuts, celery and apple and toss to coat.

○ Serve straightaway; this makes a spiky side salad!

GREEK SALAD

I know this is a fairly standard recipe, but sometimes classic flavours like these need to be celebrated. Plus, this salad is fantastically easy to assemble. Use the best ingredients you can get your hands on, as good-quality fragrant tomatoes, olives and feta will ensure a really delicious salad.

SERVES 4
VEGETARIAN

250G (8OZ) CHERRY VINE TOMATOES, SLICED IN HALF

1 CUCUMBER, UNPEELED AND SLICED

1 RED ONION, PEELED AND THINLY SLICED INTO RINGS

50G (2OZ) BLACK OLIVES (KALAMATA, IF POSSIBLE), PITTED

200G (7OZ) FETA CHEESE, CRUMBLED

A GOOD HANDFUL OF FRESH FLAT LEAF PARSLEY, ROUGHLY CHOPPED

SEA SALT AND FRESHLY GROUND BLACK PEPPER

CRUSTY BREAD, TO SERVE

DRESSING

1 TSP DRIED OREGANO

1 TBSP LEMON JUICE

1 TBSP RED WINE VINEGAR

3 TBSP EXTRA VIRGIN OLIVE OIL

- In a large bowl, whisk the ingredients for the dressing together until combined.

- Add the cherry tomatoes, cucumber, red onion and olives and toss in the dressing to coat.

- Arrange the salad on a serving plate and crumble over the feta cheese then sprinkle with chopped parsley. Season with just a little salt (the feta and olives may be salty already) and black pepper and serve straightaway with some crusty bread!

CHORIZO, ROCKET AND RED ONION SALAD

One of the first few times I visited London, I got myself down to world-famous Borough Market, where you can pick up some of the best Spanish chorizo outside Spain. Chorizo is one of my favourite ingredients; it provides delicious smoky flavours and when fried renders amazing red oil! This salad is nicest if you can get your hands on some top-quality chorizo. Don't worry if you can't get to Borough Market; you will find some excellent stuff in Spanish speciality food shops.

SERVES 4

1 GARLIC CLOVE, PEELED AND FINELY CHOPPED

JUICE OF 1/2 LEMON

1 TBSP EXTRA VIRGIN OLIVE OIL

200G (7OZ) GOOD-QUALITY CHORIZO SAUSAGE, THICKLY SLICED

1 RED ONION, PEELED, HALVED AND FINELY SLICED

40G (1½OZ) FRESH FLAT LEAF PARSLEY LEAVES

110G (4OZ) ROCKET LEAVES

CRUSTY BREAD, TO SERVE

- Whisk the garlic, lemon juice and olive oil in a large bowl and set aside.

- Fry the chorizo slices in a large frying pan over a high heat on both sides until sizzling, crispy and red. Allow the chorizo to cool slightly in the pan for 2–3 minutes, then add to the bowl together with the red onion, parsley and rocket and toss to coat in the dressing.

- Serve straightaway with some crusty bread.

GRILLED VEGETABLE SALAD WITH BASIL AND PARMESAN

This wonderfully light dish is the perfect way to enjoy some of the best summer vegetables and herbs. It doesn't skimp on flavour and will definitely fill you up. Feel free to use different types of cheese here; I sometimes make it with goat's cheese.

SERVES 4

2 TBSP OLIVE OIL, PLUS EXTRA FOR DRIZZLING

1 TBSP BALSAMIC VINEGAR

1 SMALL AUBERGINE, CUT LENGTHWAYS INTO 5MM (¼IN) SLICES

2 SMALL COURGETTE, CUT LENGTHWAYS INTO 5MM (¼IN) SLICES

6 ASPARAGUS SPEARS, ENDS SNAPPED OFF

1 RED ONION, PEELED AND CUT INTO 5MM (¼IN) SLICES

SEA SALT AND FRESHLY GROUND BLACK PEPPER

A SMALL HANDFUL OF FRESH BASIL, ROUGHLY CHOPPED

A LARGE HANDFUL OF PARMESAN CHEESE SHAVINGS

- Preheat the grill to high.

- Whisk the olive oil and balsamic vinegar together in a large bowl. Add the vegetables and toss together to coat then season with a generous pinch of salt and black pepper.

- Arrange the vegetables on a large grill tray and place under the hot grill until charred and tender. Some of vegetables will take quicker to cook than others so keep an eye on them and turn or remove as required. A ridged griddle pan set over a high heat is also very good for cooking the vegetables.

- Remove the cooked veggies and arrange on a large serving platter, sprinkle the basil and Parmesan over the top and then 'feed' the dish with a final drizzle of olive oil.

THAI BEEF AND MANGO SALAD

I am addicted to really fresh and vibrant Asian flavours like the ones in this recipe. People have mixed feelings about coriander, but I am a complete convert; it really enhances the taste of a dish like this. Slicing the beef as thinly as you can will make all the difference to every mouthful. Don't panic about having all the right veggies – if you can get the steak and the dressing sorted, the rest can vary.

SERVES 4

2 X 200G (7OZ) STRIPLOIN STEAKS

1 TBSP SESAME OIL

1 TBSP SOY SAUCE

2 GARLIC CLOVES, PEELED AND FINELY CHOPPED

SUNFLOWER OIL, FOR FRYING

150G (5OZ) BEAN SPROUTS

5 SPRING ONIONS, THINLY SLICED

1 RIPE MANGO, PEELED, STONED AND SLICED LENGTHWAYS

2 BABY GEM LETTUCES, ROUGHLY TORN

A HANDFUL OF CHOPPED PEANUTS (ABOUT 40G/1½OZ)

A HANDFUL OF FRESH MINT, ROUGHLY CHOPPED

A HANDFUL OF FRESH CORIANDER, ROUGHLY CHOPPED

DRESSING

1 TBSP SOY SAUCE

JUICE OF 1 LIME

2 TBSP FISH SAUCE (NAM PLA)

1 TBSP CASTER SUGAR

1 GARLIC CLOVE, PEELED AND FINELY CHOPPED

1 RED CHILLI, DESEEDED AND AND FINELY CHOPPED

○ In a bowl, toss the steaks in the sesame oil, soy sauce and finely chopped garlic.

○ Heat a drop of sunflower oil in a large frying pan over a high heat and just before it begins to smoke add the steaks and cook for 3–4 minutes on each side for medium rare or for an extra 2 minutes on each side for medium. Remove the steaks from the pan, place on a plate and cover with foil.

○ While the steaks are resting, prepare the dressing, whisking all the ingredients together in a large bowl. Add the bean sprouts, spring onions, mango and torn lettuce and toss to coat in the dressing.

○ Slice the cooked beef as thinly as possible, add to the salad and serve with a sprinkle of chopped peanuts, mint and coriander on top.

RED CABBAGE AND CARROT COLESLAW

Making your own coleslaw will change the way you think about it forever. In my opinion, many shops and deli bars ruin coleslaw by coating it in too much mayonnaise. By making it at home you control the ingredients and it becomes a really fresh side dish. I use one of those fantastic Magimix machines, with the slicer attachment, to get really quick results. If you don't have one, it's no big deal; it just means this recipe will take a little longer. This is the perfect accompaniment to any meat or poultry dish.

SERVES 4–6
VEGETARIAN

3 CARROTS, PEELED AND GRATED

½ HEAD OF RED CABBAGE, FINELY CHOPPED OR COARSELY GRATED

3 SPRING ONIONS, FINELY CHOPPED

1 TBSP WHOLEGRAIN MUSTARD

A GOOD PINCH OF FRESHLY GROUND BLACK PEPPER

3 TBSP MAYONNAISE (SEE PAGE 173)

- Put all the vegetables in a large bowl then add the wholegrain mustard, black pepper and mayonnaise and, using a large spoon, mix together until the veggies are evenly coated.

- Transfer the coleslaw to a large serving dish, cover with cling film and refrigerate until you are ready to serve. The coleslaw should last 2–3 days if kept in the fridge.

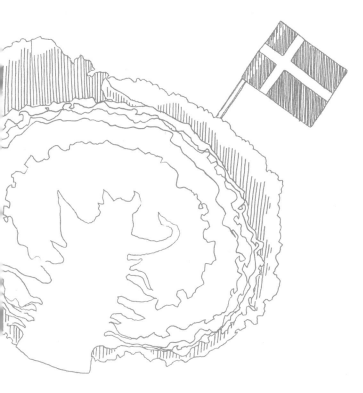

SWEDISH CABBAGE SALAD

I'm sure any Swedes who are reading this might laugh at me for including this recipe, because in Sweden it is quite commonly served at takeaway pizza restaurants! That aside, this salad is tangy and delicious and goes really well with the famous Swedish kebab pizza or with any cooked meat.

**SERVES 6-8
VEGETARIAN**

500G (1LB 2OZ) DUTCH (WHITE) CABBAGE (ABOUT ½ HEAD), THINLY SLICED

100ML (4FL OZ) SUNFLOWER OIL

4 TBSP MALT VINEGAR

1 TBSP SEA SALT

1 TBSP FRESHLY GROUND BLACK PEPPER

∘ Put the cabbage into a large bowl, add the oil, vinegar, salt and black pepper and mix until everything is combined. Taste a piece of cabbage; you may want to add another spoonful of vinegar or perhaps a little more black pepper.

∘ Cover the bowl and place in the fridge. It's best to leave the salad for at least an hour or two or even overnight. Serve cool as a tasty, healthy side dish.

COMFORT FOOD

Ah, there really is nothing like a big bowl of comfort on those dark rainy days. The recipes in this chapter are just some of my favourite dishes to produce when all I want to do is potter slowly around the kitchen, cooking up a yummy heart-warming feast! Even if most days are hectic and you can't remember what you did five minutes ago, on the rare occasion that you *do* have some free time, it's great to have a few dishes in your repertoire that can slow things down and simply allow you to enjoy the pleasure of a hearty home-cooked meal. I'm normally more of a T-shirt and shorts kinda guy than a woolly jumper fella, but I still love those days when there is nothing else to do but cook something delicious like homemade pasta, pizza, a slow-cooked stew, warming soup or a slow roast. This type of food is what my rainy days are made of.

LOVELY LAMB SHANKS WITH LENTILS

Slow-roasting lamb shanks turns the most unassuming piece of meat into a mouth-watering delicacy! The good news is that this dish takes hardly any effort to produce and once it's in the oven you can sit back and relax, safe in the knowledge that soon you will be left with delicious meat that practically falls of the bone.

SERVES 4

2 TBSP OLIVE OIL

4 LAMB SHANKS

3 ONIONS, PEELED AND FINELY CHOPPED

4 GARLIC CLOVES, PEELED AND FINELY CHOPPED

1 CARROT, PEELED AND FINELY DICED

1 CELERY STICK, FINELY SLICED

3 FRESH ROSEMARY SPRIGS

350ML (12FL OZ) RED WINE

2 X 400G TINS OF CHOPPED TOMATOES

1 TBSP BALSAMIC VINEGAR

650ML (1 PINT 3FL OZ) VEGETABLE OR BEEF STOCK

350G (12½OZ) BROWN LENTILS, RINSED

SEA SALT AND FRESHLY GROUND BLACK PEPPER

CRUSTY BREAD, TO SERVE

- Preheat the oven to 150°C (300°F), Gas mark 2.

- Heat the half the olive oil in a large flameproof casserole dish over a high heat, add the lamb shanks and cook for 4–5 minutes until browned on all sides. Remove from the casserole and set aside.

- Heat the remaining oil in the casserole, add the onions and fry for 2–3 minutes until softened but not browned. Add the garlic, carrot and celery and fry for another couple of minutes. Pop in the rosemary sprigs and stir through. Add the wine, chopped tomatoes and balsamic vinegar. Bring to the boil then reduce the heat and simmer for 5 minutes.

- Return the browned lamb shanks to the casserole and pour over the stock. Add the lentils and stir well. Do not season at this stage as salt can stop the lentils from softening. Bring to a steady simmer, then cover and cook in the oven for 3 hours until the meat is extremely tender and almost falls off the bone. Towards the end of cooking, taste and season with a good pinch of salt and black pepper.

- Serve in large deep bowls with crusty bread to soak up the juices.

Ham and Pea Soup

When I talk about using cheap cuts of meat, I don't mean that you ought to be cooking up pigs' feet or slurping down tripe! Other cheap cuts, like this ham hock, are ideal for delicious dishes like this soup. Ask your butcher for one – it shouldn't cost you more than a few quid.

SERVES 6

1 HAM HOCK (ABOUT 1.3KG/3LB)

50G (2OZ) BUTTER

1 ONION, PEELED AND FINELY CHOPPED

1KG (2¼LB) FROZEN PEAS

ABOUT 600ML (1 PINT) VEGETABLE STOCK

SEA SALT AND FRESHLY GROUND BLACK PEPPER

CRUSTY BREAD, TO SERVE

- Place the ham hock in a large, heavy-based saucepan, cover with cold water and bring to the boil, skimming off any foam that rises to the surface. Reduce the heat and simmer for about 45 minutes until the meat pulls away from the bone. (Cooking time will depend on the piece of meat, so check it with a fork: the meat is cooked when it is tender.)

- Take the ham off the heat and allow to cool in the pan. When the meat is cool, remove from the pan and reserve 600ml (1 pint) of the cooking liquid.

- Melt the butter in another large saucepan, add the onion and cook over a medium heat for 2–3 minutes until soft. Add the peas and the reserved ham liquid and stir well. Bring to the boil, then reduce the heat to a simmer and cook for 5–10 minutes until the peas are soft.

- Transfer two ladlefuls of the peas into a bowl and, using a stick blender, blitz the remaining peas in the pan until smooth. Return the whole peas to the pan and gradually add the vegetable stock. Add more stock if the soup is too thick.

- Remove the skin from the ham hock, cut up the meat and add to the soup. Reheat the soup until hot then season with a good pinch of salt and black pepper and serve with some crusty bread to make a substantial lunch.

TINK'S CHICKEN AND BROCCOLI PIE

This one comes by special request from my pal Jenny-Lee. We starred together in panto as Peter Pan and Tinkerbell a few years back, hence the name! I use ready-to-roll puff pastry for this as it is really just used as a topping. It's a handy ingredient to have in the freezer.

SERVES 4-6

75G (3OZ) BUTTER

1 LARGE ONION, PEELED, HALVED AND THINLY SLICED INTO HALF MOONS

1 HEAD OF BROCCOLI (ABOUT 300G/ 11OZ), BROKEN INTO FLORETS

2 TBSP PLAIN FLOUR, PLUS EXTRA FOR DUSTING

350ML (12FL OZ) CHICKEN STOCK

SEA SALT AND FRESHLY GROUND BLACK PEPPER

1 ROUNDED TSP ENGLISH MUSTARD

150ML (5FL OZ) SINGLE CREAM

400G (14OZ) COOKED CHICKEN, TORN INTO BITE-SIZED PIECES

350G (12$\frac{1}{2}$OZ) FROZEN PUFF PASTRY, THAWED

1 LARGE EGG, BEATEN

EQUIPMENT

A 20CM (8IN) DIAMETER BAKING DISH, ABOUT 5CM (2IN) DEEP

- Preheat the oven to 180°C (350°F), Gas mark 4.

- Melt 25g (1oz) of the butter in a large frying pan, add the onions and fry over a low heat for about 15 minutes until softened and caramelised. Remove the pan from the heat and set aside.

- Boil or steam the broccoli for 2–3 minutes until al dente (i.e. not completely tender) then drain and refresh in a bowl of iced water.

- Melt the remaining butter in a saucepan over a medium heat, add the flour and cook for 1 minute, whisking to combine. Gradually add the stock and whisk briskly until it thickens. If it goes a little lumpy, don't worry; just whisk vigorously until it becomes smooth. Reduce the heat and simmer for 3–4 minutes. Season with a generous pinch of salt and black pepper and add the mustard. Pour in the cream and stir through, allowing to cook for a further minute.

- Add the broccoli and chicken to the sauce and stir well. Transfer the mixture to the baking dish.

- Roll the pastry out on a floured work surface so that it is large enough to fit the top of the dish. Brush the edges of the dish with a little beaten egg and place the pastry on top of the pie. Crimp the edges with a fork, then brush with a little more beaten egg and cook in the oven for 25 minutes until the pastry is puffed up and golden.

Sticky Honey and Szechwan Pepper Duck

What I love about Chinese cooking is the fantastic spices that are used. I remember first coming across star anise and thinking it was one of the coolest spices I had ever seen, and that was before I had even tasted it! If you haven't used it before, don't be put off; it's really easy to prepare. Just bash it along with the peppercorns using a pestle and mortar (or a coffee grinder if you have one) until you have an aromatic powder. The combination of ingredients in this recipe makes a wonderfully sticky and delicious dish.

SERVES 2

1 TSP DARK SOY SAUCE

3 TBSP HONEY

1 TSP CHINESE RICE WINE

3 GARLIC CLOVES, PEELED AND CRUSHED

2 TSP SZECHWAN PEPPERCORNS, CRUSHED

2 STAR ANISE, CRUSHED, PLUS A FEW EXTRA WHOLE ONES

2 LARGE DUCK BREASTS, WITH SKIN ON

SWEET AND SPICY CARROT, CABBAGE AND BEAN SPROUT SALAD, TO SERVE (SEE PAGE 99)

○ In a bowl, mix the soy sauce, honey, rice wine, garlic, Szechwan peppercorns and the crushed star anise together until combined.

○ Add the duck breasts to the mixture and toss until completely coated, then cover and place in the fridge to marinate for at least 2 hours, or overnight if you have the time. Allow to come to room temperature for 10 minutes before cooking.

○ Preheat the oven to 200°C (400°F), Gas mark 6.

○ Place the duck in a roasting tray and scatter in the extra whole star anise. Cook in the oven for about 15 minutes until cooked all the way through. Baste the duck with the juices halfway through the cooking time.

○ When the duck is cooked, preheat the grill to high then place the tray under the heat for 1–2 minutes to caramelise and crisp the skin. Allow to rest for 5 minutes before cutting into thin slices and serving with a drizzle of the juices. Serve with the carrot, cabbage and bean sprout salad.

SMOKY FISH PIE

The flavours in this pie are really comforting and there is something altogether homely about the dish. I love using smoked haddock but if you're not a big fan just substitute with the regular stuff.

SERVES 4-6

900G (2LB) FLOURY POTATOES (PREFERABLY ROOSTERS), PEELED AND DICED

SEA SALT AND FRESHLY GROUND BLACK PEPPER

25G (1OZ) BUTTER

4 SPRING ONIONS, ROUGHLY CHOPPED

1 TBSP SUNFLOWER OIL

2 GARLIC CLOVES, PEELED AND FINELY CHOPPED

1 LARGE CARROT, PEELED AND FINELY CHOPPED

3 CELERY STICKS, FINELY CHOPPED

300G (11OZ) SMOKED HADDOCK FILLETS, SKINNED, BONED AND CUT INTO CHUNKS

300G (11OZ) COD FILLETS, SKINNED, BONED AND CUT INTO CHUNKS

75G (3OZ) BUTTER

75G (3OZ) PLAIN FLOUR

500ML (18FL OZ) WARM MILK

110G (4OZ) CHEDDAR CHEESE, GRATED

1 TSP DIJON MUSTARD

- Preheat the oven to 200°C (400°F), Gas mark 6.

- Place the potatoes and a good pinch of salt in a large saucepan of cold water and bring to the boil over a high heat. Reduce the heat to a simmer and cook for 12–15 minutes until tender when pierced with a fork. Drain and return the potatoes to the pan. Mash with the butter then stir through the spring onions.

- Heat the sunflower oil in a frying pan, add the garlic, carrot and celery and sauté over a medium heat for 4–5 minutes until tender. Remove the vegetables from the pan and place in a large high-sided baking dish with the haddock and cod chunks. Set aside.

- Melt the butter in another saucepan and stir in the flour quickly so you have a smooth paste. Gradually whisk in the warm milk and bring to the boil. Reduce the heat to a steady simmer and simmer for 2 minutes until the sauce thickens. Remove the pan from the heat and add three-quarters of the grated cheese (keeping the rest for the topping) and the mustard, then season with salt and black pepper. Pour the sauce over the fish and vegetables and mix to combine.

- Gently spread the mashed potato over the top, season with a little extra salt and black pepper, sprinkle on the reserved grated cheese and bake in the oven for 35–40 minutes until crisp and golden on top.

CHEESY CAULIFLOWER BAKE

This cheesy cauliflower bake is pure unashamed comfort-food indulgence! And everyone needs a bit of comfort every now and then. Don't be too scared of making the sauce – it really is so easy and literally takes minutes.

SERVES 4
VEGETARIAN

1 LARGE HEAD OF CAULIFLOWER (ABOUT 900G/2LB), BROKEN INTO FLORETS

50G (2OZ) BUTTER

50G (2OZ) PLAIN FLOUR

500ML (18FL OZ) WARM MILK

150G (5OZ) CHEDDAR CHEESE, GRATED, PLUS EXTRA FOR SPRINKLING

1 TSP DIJON MUSTARD

SEA SALT AND FRESHLY GROUND BLACK PEPPER

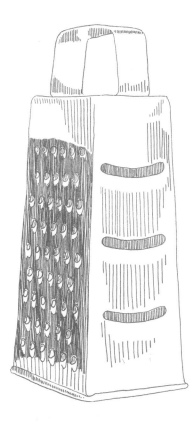

- Preheat the oven to 190°C (375°F), Gas mark 5.

- Bring a large saucepan of water to the boil, add the cauliflower florets and cook for no longer than 2–3 minutes – they should still have a good bite to them as they will finish cooking in the oven. Drain and set aside.

- Melt the butter in another saucepan and stir in the flour quickly so you have a smooth paste. Gradually whisk in the warm milk and bring to the boil. Reduce the heat to a steady simmer and simmer for 2 minutes until the sauce thickens. Remove from the heat and add the cheese and mustard then season with salt and black pepper.

- Place the cauliflower in a high-sided baking dish and pour over the cheese sauce. Top with a little extra grated cheese and another sprinkle of black pepper. Bake in the oven for 20 minutes until the top is nice and golden.

- Serve in big hefty spoonfuls and your diners will thank you for it!

SPICY WHITE BEAN AND CHORIZO SOUP

This soup is my Aunt Erica's creation and it really packs a punch. The chorizo adds great spiciness. It is even better made ahead as the flavour improves the next day.

SERVES 4-6

200G (7OZ) CHORIZO SAUSAGE, HALVED LENGTHWAYS AND SLICED

1 LARGE ONION, PEELED AND CHOPPED

225G (8OZ) CELERY, CHOPPED

300G (11OZ) CARROT, CHOPPED

2 GARLIC CLOVES, PEELED AND FINELY CHOPPED

1 TSP PAPRIKA

1 TSP CHILLI POWDER

½ TSP GROUND CUMIN

1 X 400G TIN CHOPPED TOMATOES

750ML (1 PT 6FL OZ) VEGETABLE STOCK

SEA SALT AND FRESHLY GROUND BLACK PEPPER

2 X 400G TINS CANNELLINI BEANS, DRAINED AND RINSED

CRUSTY BREAD, TO SERVE

- Fry the chorizo in a large saucepan over a high heat until it has browned and released its lovely spicy oil. Remove with a slotted spoon and set aside.

- Add the chopped onion, celery and carrots to the oil in the pan, reduce the heat and fry gently for 3-4 minutes. Add the garlic, paprika, chilli powder and cumin and fry for a further minute. Add the chopped tomatoes and stock and season with a little salt and black pepper. Stir well, return the chorizo to the pan and bring to the boil, then reduce the heat and simmer for 10 minutes.

- Finally, add the drained beans and simmer for a further 5 minutes. Serve with crusty bread.

French Onion Soup

I first tasted this soup as a kid, in a truly traditional French restaurant in Paris with big red curtains and suited and booted waiters. There are three secrets to a good French onion soup. The first is to make sure the pan is hot when you cook the onions – this will give them colour and flavour. The second is to use a really good stock: either make your own or spend a few quid extra on a good-quality one (not from a cube). The final secret is my own addition. Because I like my croûtons to be extra crunchy rather than soft and soggy, I use a good, strong sourdough bread that will sit happily on the top of the soup. For serving this, you will need six heatproof soup bowls that can go under the grill.

SERVES 6

- 2 TBSP OLIVE OIL
- 2 TBSP BUTTER
- 6 LARGE ONIONS, PEELED AND THINLY SLICED (ABOUT 700G/1½LB)
- 1 TSP SOFT DARK BROWN SUGAR
- 3 GARLIC CLOVES, PEELED AND FINELY CHOPPED
- 250ML (8½FL OZ) DRY WHITE WINE
- 1.25 LITRES (2 PINTS) BEEF, CHICKEN OR VEGETABLE STOCK
- 1 TSP DRIED THYME
- SEA SALT AND FRESHLY GROUND BLACK PEPPER
- 200G (7OZ) GRUYÈRE CHEESE (OR STRONG CHEDDAR), GRATED

CROÛTONS

- 12 SMALL OR 6 LARGE SLICES OF GOOD SOURDOUGH BREAD
- OLIVE OIL, FOR DRIZZLING
- SEA SALT
- 2 GARLIC CLOVES, PEELED

○ Heat the oil and butter in a large heavy-based saucepan over a high heat until the butter starts to bubble. Add the onions and sugar and fry, allowing the onions to catch slightly before turning them. This will help them caramelise, but be sure they don't burn. Cook for about 5 minutes until they turn a dark colour, then at this point stir in the garlic. Reduce the heat to low and cook for 30 minutes.

○ Add the white wine, stock and thyme and stir to combine with the onions. Bring to simmering point and allow to cook very slowly for a further 40 minutes. Season with salt and black pepper.

○ Meanwhile, to make the croûtons, preheat the oven to 180°C (350°F), Gas mark 4. Place the bread slices on a baking tray and drizzle both sides with olive oil. Sprinkle with salt and toast in the oven for 15 minutes until golden brown. Remove from the oven and, as soon as the toast is cool enough to touch, rub on both sides with the garlic cloves.

○ To serve, preheat the grill to medium. Ladle the soup into large bowls, place the croûton slices on top, sprinkle with the grated cheese and place under the hot grill until the cheese has melted and is bubbling and golden on top.

CHICKPEA AND PASTA TOMATO SOUP

This little dish is more than just a soup - full of lovely ingredients it tastes great and will definitely keep you going.

SERVES 4

1 TBSP OLIVE OIL

1 ONION, PEELED AND FINELY CHOPPED

3 GARLIC CLOVES, PEELED AND FINELY CHOPPED

2 CARROTS, PEELED AND FINELY DICED

3 CELERY STICKS, FINELY DICED

1 TSP DRIED OREGANO

1 X 400G TIN OF CHOPPED TOMATOES

500ML (18FL OZ) VEGETABLE STOCK

150G (5OZ) CONCHIGLETTE PASTA (OR ANY OTHER BITE-SIZED PASTA SHAPES)

1 X 400G TIN OF CHICKPEAS, DRAINED AND RINSED

SEA SALT AND FRESHLY GROUND BLACK PEPPER

25G (1OZ) PARMESAN CHEESE, GRATED, TO SERVE

° Heat the olive oil in a large saucepan over a medium heat, add the onion and garlic and fry for 3–4 minutes until soft but not browned. Add the carrots, celery and oregano and fry, stirring, until the vegetables are tender.

° Pour in the chopped tomatoes and stock and bring to the boil. Add the pasta and cook for 10–15 minutes. Add the chickpeas at the last minute and stir the soup until everything is mixed through. You want to do this just as the pasta is cooked. Season to taste with salt and black pepper.

° Serve straightaway with a little grating of Parmesan cheese on top.

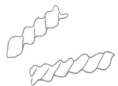

MEATBALL PASTA BAKE

I can't think of a better solution for a make-ahead dinner than this. Prep everything ahead of time, pop the dish in the fridge and only cook it when you're ready.

SERVES 4

300G (11OZ) WHOLEWHEAT PENNE

500G (1LB 2OZ) PORK MINCE

1 ONION, PEELED AND FINELY CHOPPED

1 TSP DRIED OREGANO

2 GARLIC CLOVES, PEELED AND FINELY CHOPPED

2 TSP DIJON MUSTARD

1 TBSP TOMATO KETCHUP

1 TBSP WORCESTERSHIRE SAUCE

SEA SALT AND FRESHLY GROUND BLACK PEPPER

75-100G (3-3½OZ) CHEDDAR CHEESE, GRATED

GREEN SALAD, TO SERVE

SAUCE

1 TBSP OLIVE OIL

1 ONION, PEELED AND FINELY CHOPPED

2 GARLIC CLOVES, PEELED AND FINELY CHOPPED

2 X 400G TINS OF CHOPPED TOMATOES

50ML (2FL OZ) RED WINE

2 TSP DRIED OREGANO

1 TSP GRANULATED SUGAR

SEA SALT AND FRESHLY GROUND BLACK PEPPER

- Cook the pasta in a large saucepan according to the instructions on the packet, then drain and set aside in the pan.

- Preheat the grill to medium.

- In a large bowl, combine the pork with the onion, oregano, garlic, Dijon mustard, tomato ketchup, Worcestershire sauce and a good pinch of salt and black pepper. Form the mixture into 28-30 bite-sized meatballs and arrange on a grill tray. Cook under the hot grill for 10-12 minutes, turning occasionally, until browned on all sides.

- For the sauce, heat the oil in another saucepan over a medium heat, add the onion and gently fry for 1-2 minutes. Add the garlic and fry for a further 30-40 seconds. Add the chopped tomatoes, wine, oregano and sugar, then season with salt and black pepper. Bring to the boil, lower the heat and simmer for 15 minutes until the sauce has reduced.

- Preheat the oven to 200°C (400°F), Gas mark 6.

- Pour the sauce over the cooked pasta and add the meatballs. Stir until everything is combined, then transfer to a high-sided baking dish. Sprinkle grated cheese over the top and place in the oven to bake for 30 minutes.

- Serve in big hearty portions with a green side salad.

SIMPLE GARLIC AND ROSEMARY ROAST LAMB

Most meat really benefits from the roasting process and lamb is no different. When it's in season, lamb needs very little work to bring out its fantastic natural flavours. Roasting it with the classic combination of rosemary and garlic is simply the only way to go, in my book. You get delicious, mouth-watering results and a kitchen filled with amazing aromas.

SERVES 6–8

1 LEG OF LAMB, BONED AND ROLLED

A FEW FRESH ROSEMARY SPRIGS

A FEW GARLIC CLOVES, PEELED AND SLICED INTO THICK SPIKES

OLIVE OIL, FOR DRIZZLING

SEA SALT AND FRESHLY GROUND BLACK PEPPER

250ML (8½FL OZ) LAMB STOCK (OR USE BEEF OR VEGETABLE IF YOU ARE STUCK)

TO SERVE

ROAST POTATOES

STEAMED ASPARAGUS

- Preheat the oven to 180°C (350°F), Gas mark 4.

- Place the lamb in a large roasting tray and, using the point of a sharp knife, make holes all over the lamb 2–3cm (¾–1¼in) apart. Insert some rosemary sprigs and a spike of garlic in each hole. Drizzle with a little olive oil and season generously with sea salt and black pepper.

- Roast in the oven and, depending on the weight of the leg, for 25–30 minutes per 450g (1lb) for medium rare. Alternatively, check the lamb with a meat thermometer; it should be 60–65°C (140–150°F) for medium rare. Transfer the cooked lamb to a serving dish, cover with foil and allow to rest for 10–15 minutes.

- Tip the juices to one corner of the roasting tray and spoon the fat off the top with a metal spoon. Place the tray on the hob and add the stock. Bring to the boil and whisk the gravy, making sure to incorporate all the caramelised meat juices from the base and sides of the tray. If you want a thicker sauce, you can add a little roux (equal amounts of butter and flour mixed together) while it comes to the boil. Decant to a small gravy jug.

- Serve slices of lamb with a little of the gravy, some roast potatoes and steamed asparagus.

ROAST GARLIC BANGERS AND MASH

Ah, mash! It never fails to make me feel at home. Piping hot, salty and incredibly creamy, it's something I could eat all day long. This is one of my absolute favourite ways of enjoying it, with some roughly mashed roast garlic mixed through – it's heaven on a plate. The trick is to get your hands on some top-quality sausages, which you should be able to pick up at good butchers or supermarkets.

SERVES 4

2 GARLIC BULBS, UNPEELED

3 TBSP OLIVE OIL

SEA SALT AND FRESHLY GROUND BLACK PEPPER

1KG (2¼LB) FLOURY POTATOES, PEELED AND DICED

A GENEROUS KNOB OF BUTTER

75ML (3FL OZ) HOT MILK

8 LARGE GOOD-QUALITY SAUSAGES OR 4 LARGE BANGERS

∘ First things first – get the garlic in the oven. Preheat the oven to 200°C (400°F), Gas mark 6.

∘ Slice the top of each garlic bulb just enough so that each of the cloves is exposed and place in a roasting tray. Drizzle with 2 tablespoons of the olive oil and season with some salt. Roast in the oven for 40 minutes until soft and tender. Remove the roasted cloves from their skins and mash with the back of a fork.

∘ Meanwhile, place the potatoes in a large saucepan of cold water and bring to the boil over a high heat. Reduce the heat and simmer gently for 10–15 minutes until tender when pierced with a fork. Drain the potatoes, return them to the pan and add the butter and hot milk. Using a potato masher, mash until smooth and creamy. You may want to add a little bit more or less milk and butter – it is up to you. Add the mashed garlic and season with salt and black pepper, stirring to combine. Cover with a lid and keep warm while you cook the sausages.

∘ Heat the remaining olive oil in a large frying pan over a high heat and fry the sausages for 7–8 minutes until cooked through and golden brown.

∘ Serve the mash topped with the cooked sausages and tuck in.

Swedish Meatballs with Dill Spring Potatoes

These have been made world-famous by IKEA, where they serve them in the food hall. However, unless you have tried the homemade version, I personally think you haven't properly tasted this traditional Swedish dish. I have to admit I was a little put off when I was first served them with a big dollop of jam on the side, but I was quickly converted and now I'm convinced these meatballs have to be served with lingonsylt (lingonberry jam) in order to be truly authentic.

SERVES 4

250G (9OZ) BEEF MINCE

150G (5OZ) PORK MINCE

2 TBSP FRESH WHITE BREADCRUMBS

1 SMALL ONION, PEELED AND FINELY CHOPPED

1 LARGE EGG, LIGHTLY BEATEN

SEA SALT AND FRESHLY GROUND BLACK PEPPER

50G (3OZ) BUTTER

750G (1LB 10OZ) BABY POTATOES

A FEW FRESH DILL SPRIGS, ROUGHLY CHOPPED

1 TBSP PLAIN FLOUR

200ML (7FL OZ) MILK

LINGONBERRY JAM, TO SERVE (AVAILABLE IN SPECIALITY SWEDISH FOOD STORES)

- Combine the minced beef and pork in a bowl with the breadcrumbs, onion and egg. Season with a generous pinch of salt and black pepper and form into 24 bite-sized meatballs.

- Place the potatoes in a large saucepan of cold water and bring to the boil over a high heat. Reduce the heat to a simmer and cook for 10–15 minutes until tender when pierced with a fork. Drain the potatoes, return them to the pan and toss with half the butter and the chopped dill. Put a lid on the pan to keep the potatoes warm, then set aside.

- Meanwhile, melt the remaining butter in a large frying pan until foaming and fry the meatballs for 10–12 minutes, turning occasionally, until cooked through and browned all over. Remove the meatballs from the pan, place on a warm plate, cover and set aside.

- Add the flour to the hot butter and crusty bits still in the pan (add a little more butter if needed) and whisk to combine. Still whisking, add the milk, a little at a time, until it is all combined. Simmer for 2–3 minutes until the sauce has thickened then season with salt and black pepper.

- Serve the meatballs with the sauce, a few dill spring potatoes and a hearty dollop of lingonberry jam.

BLUE CHEESE AND RED ONION QUICHE

Time for me to fess up: it's only in the last few years that I've grown to love and appreciate cheese. Throughout my teens I would steer clear of the stuff until my pal Izzy, from Sheridans Cheesemongers in Dublin, insisted it was the way forward. The strong flavour of blue cheese stands up nicely in this quiche, complemented by the sweetness of the caramelised onion. I use Cashel Blue but any other blue cheese will do.

SERVES 6-8
VEGETARIAN

225G (8OZ) PLAIN FLOUR,
  PLUS EXTRA FOR DUSTING

A PINCH OF SALT

125G (4½OZ) COLD BUTTER,
  CUT INTO PIECES

GREEN SALAD, TO SERVE

FILLING

2 TBSP OLIVE OIL

4 LARGE RED ONIONS, PEELED,
  HALVED AND SLICED INTO HALF MOONS

SEA SALT AND FRESHLY GROUND
  BLACK PEPPER

3 LARGE EGGS

300ML (10½FL OZ) DOUBLE CREAM

150G (5OZ) CASHEL BLUE CHEESE,
  CRUMBLED

A FEW FRESH THYME SPRIGS,
  LEAVES ONLY

EQUIPMENT

A 28CM (11IN) QUICHE OR TART TIN
  WITH A REMOVABLE BASE

- To make the filling, heat the olive oil in a frying pan, add the onions and fry over a low-medium heat for 10–15 minutes until soft and caramelised. Season with salt and black pepper then remove from the heat and allow to cool. This can be done ahead of time.

- To make the pastry, place the flour and salt in a large bowl. Add the butter and, using your fingertips, rub the butter into the flour until the mixture resembles rough breadcrumbs. Sprinkle over 1–2 tablespoons of water and bring the dough together to form a ball. Wrap the dough in cling film and place in the fridge to rest for at least 10 minutes.

- Preheat the oven to 180°C (350°F), Gas mark 4 and place a baking tray on the middle shelf. Roll out the pastry on a lightly floured work surface and use to line the quiche tin. Prick the base with a fork and place on the baking tray in the oven for about 15 minutes until lightly golden.

- In a bowl, whisk the eggs and cream together until combined. Arrange the caramelised onions on the base of the cooked pastry case, scatter over the crumbled cheese and the thyme leaves and season with salt and black pepper.

- Gently pour the egg and cream mixture into the pastry case and bake in the oven for 30–35 minutes until the filling is set and golden on top. Allow to cool then serve hot or cold slices with a green salad.

Basic Thin-crust Pizza

This recipe creates a wonderfully thin, crisp, yet still chewy dough which ticks all the boxes for me. You can easily freeze the dough once it has finished rising – just punch it down and pop in a freezer bag. Take it out the day before you plan to use it and allow to it to defrost in the fridge.

MAKES 3–4 THIN BASES
VEGETARIAN

**250G (9OZ) PLAIN FLOUR,
  PLUS EXTRA FOR DUSTING**

**1 X 7.5G SACHET OF EASY-BLEND
  DRIED YEAST**

½ TSP SALT

**1 TBSP EXTRA VIRGIN OLIVE OIL,
  PLUS EXTRA FOR OILING**

BASIC TOPPING

**ABOUT 3 TBSP TOMATO SAUCE PER
  PIZZA (FROM A JAR, OR SEE PAGE
  142 BUT OMIT THE CHILLI)**

**175G (6OZ) MOZZARELLA CHEESE,
  GRATED**

- In a large bowl, combine the flour, easy-blend yeast and salt. Make a well in the flour and pour in 175ml (6fl oz) of tepid water and the olive oil. Using your fingertips, slowly bring the flour in from the sides and continue to mix until a rough dough forms.

- Turn the dough out on a floured work surface and knead for about 5 minutes. If the dough is too sticky add a little extra flour until it becomes smooth. Form the dough into a ball and place in a clean oiled bowl. Cover with a damp tea towel or cling film and set aside in a warm spot for about 45 minutes or until the dough has doubled in size.

- Punch the dough down on a lightly floured work surface then knead again for a minute and place back in the bowl to rise for a further 10 minutes.

- Preheat the oven to 200°C (400°F), Gas mark 6.

- Divide the dough into 3–4 pieces and roll out into very thin rounds. Sprinkle flour onto a baking sheet and place a pizza base on it. Spread the base with tomato sauce and sprinkle with mozzarella or add your chosen toppings (see overleaf).

- Bake in the oven for 10–15 minutes until the cheese turns golden and the crust becomes crisp. Serve straightaway.

ROCKET, GOAT'S CHEESE AND RED ONION PIZZA

SERVES 1–2
VEGETARIAN

1 PIZZA BASE (SEE PAGE 139)

1 TBSP EXTRA VIRGIN OLIVE OIL, PLUS EXTRA FOR DRIZZLING

2 RED ONIONS, PEELED, HALVED AND SLICED IN HALF MOONS

ABOUT 3 TBSP TOMATO SAUCE

75G (3OZ) GOAT'S CHEESE LOG, SLICED

A GOOD HANDFUL OF ROCKET LEAVES (OPTIONAL)

○ Preheat the oven to 200°C (400°F), Gas mark 6.

○ Heat the olive oil in a large frying pan over a low heat, add the onion and cook for 5–7 minutes until caramelised.

○ Assemble the pizza by spreading the tomato sauce over the base, then adding the caramelised onions and the slices of goat's cheese.

○ Bake in the oven for 10–15 minutes then serve straightaway with a handful of rocket scattered on the top, if you wish, and a final drizzle of olive oil.

CHORIZO, BASIL AND OLIVE PIZZA

SERVES 1–2

1 PIZZA BASE (SEE PAGE 139)

ABOUT 3 TBSP TOMATO SAUCE

30G (1¼OZ) CHORIZO SAUSAGE, SLICED

75G (3OZ) MOZZARELLA CHEESE, GRATED

30G (1¼OZ) GREEN OLIVES, PITTED

A GOOD HANDFUL OF FRESH BASIL, ROUGHLY CHOPPED

○ Preheat the oven to 200°C (400°F), Gas mark 6.

○ Assemble the pizza by spreading the tomato sauce over the base then adding the chorizo slices, mozzarella and green olives.

○ Bake in the oven for 10–15 minutes and serve straightaway with a sprinkle of basil.

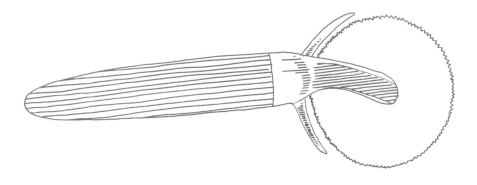

GET DRESSED AFTER PIZZA!

SERVES 1–2

- 1 PIZZA BASE (SEE PAGE 139)
- ABOUT 3 TBSP TOMATO SAUCE
- 75G (3OZ) MOZZARELLA CHEESE, GRATED
- 50G (2OZ) PROSCIUTTO, SLICED
- 1 TBSP OLIVE OIL
- 1 TSP BALSAMIC VINEGAR
- 25G (1OZ) BABY SPINACH LEAVES
- 25G (1OZ) ROCKET LEAVES
- 15G (½OZ) PARMESAN CHEESE, SHAVED

- Preheat the oven to 200°C (400°F), Gas mark 6.

- Assemble the pizza by spreading the tomato sauce over the base then adding the mozzarella and slices of prosciutto.

- Whisk the olive oil and balsamic vinegar in a bowl, add the spinach and rocket and toss until until coated. Set aside.

- Bake the pizza in the oven for 10–15 minutes and serve straightaway with a handful of the dressed leaves and some Parmesan shavings.

NICE AND SPICY PIZZA

SERVES 1–2

- 1 PIZZA BASE (SEE PAGE 139)
- ABOUT 3 TBSP TOMATO SAUCE
- 50G (2OZ) MOZZARELLA CHEESE, TORN
- 30G (1¼OZ) PEPPERONI SLICES
- 15G (½OZ) GREEN JALAPEÑO PEPPERS FROM A JAR, DRAINED AND ROUGHLY CHOPPED

- Preheat the oven to 200°C (400°F), Gas mark 6.

- Assemble the pizza by spreading the tomato sauce over the base then adding the torn mozzarella, pepperoni slices and chopped jalepeño peppers.

- Bake in the oven for 10–15 minutes and serve straightaway.

HOMEMADE GNOCCHI IN A SPICY TOMATO SAUCE

Gnocchi are my secret comfort-food fix. I first tasted these little lumps of goodness while in Boston visiting my friend Lisa, whose Italian grandmamma makes all her own pasta and produced a delicious bowl of homemade gnocchi for me. I like to think of it as 'clumsy pasta', because it's so easy to make. This recipe will give you a proper taste of Italia.

SERVES 4-6

500G (1LB 2OZ) FLOURY POTATOES (PREFERABLY ROOSTER), PEELED (ABOUT 4 MEDIUM)

200G (7OZ) PLAIN FLOUR, PLUS EXTRA FOR DUSTING

1 LARGE EGG

1 TSP DRIED OREGANO

SEA SALT AND FRESHLY GROUND BLACK PEPPER

PARMESAN CHEESE SHAVINGS, TO SERVE

SPICY TOMATO SAUCE

1 TBSP OLIVE OIL

2 GARLIC CLOVES, PEELED AND FINELY CHOPPED

1 SMALL ONION, PEELED AND FINELY CHOPPED

½ TSP DRIED CHILLI FLAKES

1 TSP DRIED OREGANO

2 X 400G TINS OF CHOPPED TOMATOES

75ML (3FL OZ) RED WINE

SEA SALT AND FRESHLY GROUND BLACK PEPPER

1 TSP GRANULATED SUGAR (OPTIONAL)

- Place the potatoes in a large saucepan of cold water and bring to the boil. Reduce the heat to a simmer and cook for 20 minutes or until soft when pierced with a fork. Drain and peel when cool enough to handle.

- Meanwhile, make the sauce. Heat the oil in a large frying pan over a medium-high heat, add the garlic and onion and fry for 3–4 minutes until soft. Stir in the dried chilli and oregano and fry until you can smell the aromatics! Add the tomatoes and wine, bring to the boil then lower the heat and simmer for 15 minutes until reduced. Season with salt and black pepper. You may want to add a teaspoon of sugar if the tomatoes are a little too acidic.

- Return the potatoes to the pan they were cooked in and mash until really smooth. Add the flour, egg, oregano and a generous amount of salt and black pepper. Mix to a dough, then turn out onto a floured work surface and knead gently for 2–3 minutes.

- Divide the dough into four and roll each piece into a sausage, about 50cm (20in) long. Cut each sausage into 15 pieces and, using the tines of a fork, press each piece gently to shape the gnocchi, leaving a dent from your thumb or finger on one side and fork marks on top. Put on a floured plate and continue to shape the rest.

- Cook the gnocchi, in batches, in a pan of salted boiling water for 2 minutes or until they rise to the surface. Lift out with a slotted spoon and serve with the spicy tomato sauce (reheated if necessary), a sprinkle of black pepper and Parmesan shavings.

STRETCH YOUR MEALS

There are many ways to make life easier in the kitchen and using leftovers is one of them. Every cook will find themselves with odds and ends left over, so it is useful to know what to do with them. My mum was, and still is, the queen of all things left over. The big joke in our family was that we should never mention if we really liked a particular dish, because invariably she would cook it again but this time with double quantities so that she could serve it up for a few days running! Although I complained about it as a kid, now I really love using leftovers and there are some truly fantastic recipes that can be produced from them. In this chapter I have come up with four different ideas for each main ingredient. Some of the recipes use leftovers; others are based solely on the ingredients you are most likely to have in your kitchen. They are recipes that are meant to inspire you, rather than to be followed to the letter; after all, that's the way I learned to cook. One of the hardest things I had to learn when I first began writing recipes was to start measuring things accurately. I was far more used to pouring in a hearty splash of red wine or adding a hefty handful of fresh basil than to working out the exact quantity in millilitres or grams. So don't feel you have to stick too rigidly to the weights, and do have the confidence to experiment a bit – if I suggest a particular ingredient and you don't have it to hand, think of a substitute and go for it!

CHICKEN

Chicken is a big part of most people's diets and many families like a good roast chicken on a Sunday, but the beauty of this bird is that it leaves super leftovers. You can make great homemade chicken stock from the bones; it can be frozen or kept in the fridge to be added to soups and sauces to pump up the flavours. And you can't beat a great leftover chicken sambo the day after the bird has been roasted. Here are some of my favourite ways to get the best out of a good chicken.

Simple Roast Chicken

Mastering a really good roast chicken is a bit of an art form in itself and the basis of any home cook's reputation. I love cooking it so that you have a salty, crispy skin and meat that is moist and full of herby, aromatic flavour.

SERVES 6

2 TBSP OLIVE OIL

A FEW FRESH ROSEMARY SPRIGS

A FEW FRESH THYME SPRIGS

4 GARLIC CLOVES, PEELED

1 LARGE CHICKEN

SEA SALT AND FRESHLY GROUND
  BLACK PEPPER

° Preheat the oven to 200°C (400°F), Gas mark 6.

° Blitz together the olive oil, rosemary, thyme and garlic cloves using a pestle and mortar or a hand-held blender until you get a smooth paste.

° Slather the chicken in the super green herby garlic paste, season with a generous pinch of salt and black pepper and then roast in the oven for 45–50 minutes until cooked through and the juices run clear when a skewer is inserted into the thickest part of the thigh.

° Remove the chicken from the oven and allow to rest for 15 minutes, covered in foil, before serving, remembering to save any juices that run off, to use for other things, such as gravy (see page 131).

Basic Chicken Stock

Not only is a good hearty chicken stock packed with health benefits, but it can also be the base for hundreds of different quick and simple recipes. It freezes extremely well in resealable plastic bags for up to three months and can be defrosted just before you need it. I sometimes ladle stock into ice-cube trays, then throw the frozen cubes into sauces for extra flavour.

MAKES ABOUT 3 LITRES (5½ PINTS)

LEFTOVER BONES AND CARCASS OF 1 COOKED CHICKEN (SEE PAGE 146)

175ML (6FL OZ) WHITE WINE

1 ONION, PEELED AND CHOPPED

1 LARGE CARROT, PEELED AND SLICED

1 LARGE LEEK, TRIMMED AND SLICED

1 CELERY STICK, CHOPPED

3 PARSLEY STALKS

8 BLACK PEPPERCORNS

∘ Place all the ingredients in a large saucepan, pour in 6 litres (10½ pints) of water and bring to a steady boil. Reduce the heat and allow to simmer gently for 3 hours or until the flavour is right for you. Make sure every now and then to skim any fat and scum that rises to the surface. This will ensure you have a nice clear stock. Strain the stock and allow to cool.

∘ The stock can be kept in the fridge for a few days or frozen for later use.

Ultimate Roast Chicken Salad

As I've said, there is no better leftover food than roast chicken, and I personally think it tastes much better a day or two after it's cooked because the flavours really develop. That is, if it lasts that long! This salad is a great way to enjoy the delicious leftover meat and will most definitely leave you full and satisfied.

SERVES 4

125G (4½OZ) PANCETTA BITS

1 CIABATTA, SLICED INTO THICK SLICES

OLIVE OIL, FOR DRIZZLING

2 GARLIC CLOVES, PEELED
AND CUT IN HALF

1 X QUANTITY CREAMY CHIVE DRESSING
(SEE PAGE 180)

1 COS LETTUCE, TORN INTO
CHUNKY BITE-SIZED PIECES

400G (14OZ) COOKED CHICKEN PIECES
(A SMALL HANDFUL PER PERSON)

A GOOD HANDFUL OF PARMESAN
CHEESE SHAVINGS PER PERSON

SEA SALT AND FRESHLY
GROUND BLACK PEPPER

- In a frying pan, cook the pancetta over a medium heat for 3–5 minutes until crisp and browned. Place on a plate lined with kitchen paper and set aside.

- Drizzle the ciabatta slices generously with olive oil and place in the frying pan to toast until golden brown on each side. Remove the ciabatta from the pan and rub the garlic cloves on both sides then cut the toast into thick chunks.

- Place the dressing in a large bowl, add the lettuce leaves, chicken pieces (warmed if you want) and ciabatta soldiers and toss until everything is evenly coated in the dressing.

- Sprinkle the Parmesan shavings and pancetta over the top and season the salad with salt and a good grinding of black pepper. Serve straightaway.

Moroccan Chicken Tagine

I use chicken thighs for this recipe as they are quite inexpensive, but feel free to substitute with chicken breasts if you need to. If you have the time, do marinate the chicken pieces in the spice mixture overnight, as it makes all the difference to the overall taste. I also find that the tagine really develops in flavour the day after cooking, making any leftovers a delicious quick-fix lunch for the following day.

SERVES 4

1 TSP GROUND GINGER

1 TSP FRESHLY GROUND BLACK PEPPER

1 TSP TURMERIC

½ TSP CAYENNE PEPPER

2 TSP PAPRIKA

10 CHICKEN THIGHS, SKINNED, BONED AND CUT IN HALF

50G (2OZ) DRIED APRICOTS, FINELY SLICED

50G (2OZ) SULTANAS

1 TBSP SUNFLOWER OIL

2 ONIONS, PEELED AND ROUGHLY CHOPPED

8 GARLIC CLOVES, PEELED AND FINELY CHOPPED

1 TBSP HONEY

2 X 400G TINS OF CHOPPED TOMATOES

½ TBSP VEGETABLE BOUILLON POWDER

250G (9OZ) COUSCOUS

A HANDFUL OF FRESH CORIANDER, ROUGHLY CHOPPED, TO SERVE

° Mix all the spices together in a small bowl. Place the chicken pieces in a large bowl, add half the spice mixture and toss until the chicken pieces are thoroughly coated. Cover and place in the fridge for 1–2 hours to allow the spices to permeate the meat.

° Place the apricots and sultanas in a bowl and cover them with boiling water.

° Heat the oil in a large high-sided frying pan over a high heat, add the marinated chicken pieces and fry until browned all over. Remove the chicken from the pan and set aside.

° Add the onions and garlic to the pan and fry for 1 minute over a low heat, then add the remaining spice mixture and fry until the onions are soft. Add the apricots and sultanas and the soaking liquid, along with the honey, chopped tomatoes and bouillon powder. Bring to the boil, then reduce the heat and simmer for 15 minutes until the sauce has reduced and thickened. Add the chicken pieces and toss until coated in the sauce then cook gently for 20 minutes until the chicken is cooked through.

° Prepare the couscous according to instruction on the packet and serve with the chicken, sprinkled generously with chopped coriander. This is also good served with bulgur wheat (see page 39).

MEAT SPICE RUBS

Meat spice rubs suit fatty pieces of meat or meat on the bone. The rubs are super to make ahead of time – simply mix all the ingredients together – and will sit nicely in jars.for a few months, ready to use whenever needed. Rub them into any meat to give it great flavour, then just cook as normal.

INDIAN

- -
4 TBSP CURRY POWDER
- -
1 TBSP SEA SALT
- -
1 TBSP GROUND CUMIN
- -
1 TBSP GROUND CORIANDER
- -
1 TBSP TURMERIC
- -
1 TBSP GROUND GINGER
- -

HERB SALT RUB

- -
1 TBSP DRIED OREGANO
- -
A FEW FRESH ROSEMARY SPRIGS,
  ROUGHLY CHOPPED
- -
A FEW FRESH THYME SPRIGS,
  ROUGHLY CHOPPED
- -
2 TBSP SEA SALT
- -
1 TBSP FRESHLY GROUND BLACK PEPPER

CAJUN

- -
1 TBSP PAPRIKA
- -
1 TBSP CAYENNE PEPPER
- -
1 TSP GARLIC SALT
- -
1 TSP DRIED ENGLISH MUSTARD
- -
1 TSP DRIED OREGANO
- -
1/2 TSP FRESHLY GROUND BLACK PEPPER

ASIAN

- -
2 TBSP CHINESE FIVE SPICE POWDER
- -
1 TBSP SOFT DARK BROWN SUGAR
- -
1 TBSP SEA SALT
- -
1 TSP DRIED CHILLI FLAKES
- -

Pasta

Pasta is definitely one of my favourite quick-fix kitchen cupboard ingredients. It's fairly inexpensive and can easily feed a crowd. I generally go for the wholewheat variety as it has many health benefits and, in my opinion, more flavour. If you are hooked on the white version, do give the wholewheat a try and you might be surprised. I like to cook a big batch of pasta at the start of the week, adding ingredients here and there for tasty dinners and quick on-the-go lunches. These are just four of my favourite ways with pasta, but what you do with it is totally up to you.

PESTO PASTA

This was one of the first Italian recipes I learned to make. It's a fantastic combination of tastes and textures, providing fresh, creamy, nutty, salty flavours, all rolled into one mega mouthful. The good news is that it's super easy to throw together and perfect to make during the summer, when your basil will hopefully be thriving on a sunny windowsill.

SERVES 4

300G (11OZ) WHOLEWHEAT PENNE

25G (1OZ) TOASTED PINE NUTS (SEE PAGE 61), PLUS EXTRA TO SERVE

1 GARLIC CLOVE, PEELED

50G (2OZ) FRESH BASIL LEAVES

25G (1OZ) PARMESAN CHEESE, GRATED, PLUS EXTRA TO SERVE

75ML (3FL OZ) EXTRA VIRGIN OLIVE OIL, PLUS EXTRA FOR DRIZZLING

SEA SALT AND FRESHLY GROUND BLACK PEPPER

- Cook the pasta in a large saucepan according to the instructions on the packet, then drain.

- Meanwhile, using a pestle and mortar or a food processor, blitz the pine nuts, garlic, basil, Parmesan and olive oil until you have a smooth paste. Season with salt and black pepper

- Stir the pesto sauce over the hot, cooked pasta and serve with an extra sprinkle of pine nuts and grated Parmesan and a drizzle of olive oil. Perfection in a bowl.

SLOW-ROAST TOMATO, BASIL AND GOAT'S CHEESE PASTA

It's great to know a couple of really easy recipes that you can turn to when you don't feel like cooking. With maximum results for minimum effort, this is my favourite. Use whatever pasta shapes you like.

SERVES 4
VEGETARIAN

300G (11OZ) WHOLEWHEAT PASTA

75G (3OZ) GOAT'S CHEESE, CRUMBLED

A GOOD HANDFUL OF FRESH
  BASIL LEAVES

1 QUANTITY OF SLOW-ROASTED
  CHERRY TOMATOES (SEE PAGE 77)

SEA SALT AND FRESHLY GROUND
  BLACK PEPPER

○ Cook the pasta in a large saucepan according to the instructions on the packet. Drain the pasta and return to the pan.

○ While the pasta is still hot, stir through the goat's cheese, basil and slow-roasted cherry tomatoes. Season with a good pinch of salt and black pepper and serve immediately.

CREAMY SMOKED SALMON AND SUN-BLUSHED TOMATO TAGLIATELLE

This is a great meal to throw together in just minutes and it's really filling. You can pick up sun-blushed tomatoes in the supermarket. They are a much brighter colour than sun-dried tomatoes and a little less intense in flavour.

SERVES 4

300G (11OZ) TAGLIATELLE

2 TBSP OLIVE OIL

2 GARLIC CLOVES, PEELED AND FINELY CHOPPED

200G (7OZ) LOW FAT CRÈME FRAÎCHE

A GOOD HANDFUL OF FRESH DILL, CHOPPED

75G (3OZ) SUN-BLUSHED TOMATOES, ROUGHLY CHOPPED

SEA SALT AND FRESHLY GROUND BLACK PEPPER

200G (7OZ) SLICED SMOKED SALMON, CUT INTO STRIPS

JUICE OF ½ LEMON, TO SERVE

○ Cook the pasta in a large saucepan according to the instructions on the packet, then drain.

○ Heat the oil in a large frying pan over a low-medium heat, add the garlic and fry gently for 1 minute. Add the crème fraîche and heat through then add the dill, tomatoes and a good pinch of salt and black pepper and stir through.

○ Finally add the salmon strips and hot tagliatelle and toss everything together until coated. Serve each portion with a generous squeeze of lemon juice.

ROCKET-FUELLED PASTA WITH AVOCADO AND PARMESAN

Avocados are packed with vitamins and other healthy nutrients, so all the more reason to eat them. Look for avocados which are slightly soft to the touch when you press them with your fingers. And remember that, once cut, they don't tend to like sitting around and will discolour quickly, so always prepare them last and give them a spritz of lemon juice to keep them fresh for as long as possible.

SERVES 4

300G (11OZ) WHOLEWHEAT PENNE

75G (3OZ) ROCKET LEAVES, ROUGHLY CHOPPED

50G (2OZ) BABY SPINACH LEAVES

A GOOD HANDFUL OF FRESHLY GRATED PARMESAN CHEESE

1 GARLIC CLOVE, PEELED AND CRUSHED

1 TSP BALSAMIC VINEGAR

2 TBSP EXTRA VIRGIN OLIVE OIL

2 AVOCADOS,

JUICE OF 1 LEMON

SEA SALT AND FRESHLY GROUND BLACK PEPPER

○ Cook the pasta in a large saucepan according the instructions on the packet.

○ Meanwhile, add the rocket, spinach, Parmesan and garlic to a large bowl and set aside.

○ When the pasta is cooked, drain and add it to the bowl. Pour in the balsamic vinegar and olive oil and stir until the pasta is coated.

○ Peel and stone the avocados, then slice and spritz with lemon juice. Add to the pasta, season with a good pinch of salt and black pepper, and add an extra sprinkle of cheese. Serve straightaway and devour.

EGGS

Some people think meals with eggs as the base ingredient can be a little boring, but I disagree; there are so many things you can do with them. I always buy eggs in bulk for fear of running out, which has meant coming up with some inventive recipes to get through a glut. I love eggs for breakfast, and I have a number of different recipes to make them extra special. Most of them I could probably eat throughout the day regardless of their breakfast connotations – so why not try them yourself, whatever mood you're in.

BREAKFAST EGG PARCELS

Served as a breakfast for two, these egg parcels look as impressive as they taste.

SERVES 2

1 TBSP OLIVE OIL

2 GARLIC CLOVES, PEELED AND FINELY CHOPPED

50G (2OZ) BABY SPINACH LEAVES

6 RASHERS OF PANCETTA (ABOUT 90G/3½OZ), SLICED LENGTHWAYS

75G (3OZ) GOAT'S CHEESE, CRUMBLED

4 LARGE EGGS

FRESHLY GROUND BLACK PEPPER

TOASTED CRUSTY SOURDOUGH BREAD, TO SERVE

EQUIPMENT

A 6-HOLE MUFFIN TRAY

○ Preheat the oven to 200°C (400°F), Gas mark 6.

○ Heat the oil in a large frying pan over a medium heat, add the garlic and fry for 30 seconds. Add the spinach and cook until it has wilted. Remove the pan from the heat and set aside.

○ Line four of the muffin tray hollows with the slices of pancetta. Add a spoonful of the spinach and garlic mix to each hollow and top with a little goat's cheese. Crack an egg into each hollow and add a generous pinch of black pepper. Bake in the oven for 10 minutes until the white of each egg is set and the yolk still a little soft.

○ Serve with some toasted crusty sourdough bread and enjoy for a hefty breakfast.

MY PERFECT SCRAMBLED EGGS

There are a few everyday dishes that, once you get them right, you will never forget how to do them. These are my perfect scrambled eggs, good enough to solve all of life's little problems! I had scrambled eggs served with chilli jam at Rosie's café in Brixton, London. It was a great little addition on the side, so I totally recommend it.

SERVES 1
VEGETARIAN

1 WHOLEMEAL BAGEL, HALVED

2 LARGE EGGS

SEA SALT AND FRESHLY
GROUND BLACK PEPPER

A SMALL KNOB OF BUTTER

CHILLI JAM, TO SERVE

○ Place the bagel halves in a toaster and toast until golden brown.

○ Whisk the eggs with a little salt, black pepper and the butter, then pour the mixture into a small non-stick saucepan. Place the saucepan over a low heat and allow the eggs to cook gently until they start to set. Using a wooden spoon, slowly pull the eggs towards the centre. Keep the mixture moving until you have really creamy scrambled eggs. Make sure not to overcook the eggs – take them off the heat while they are still slightly runny and creamy. It's a balance to judge but when you taste them you'll know what I mean.

○ Spoon the scrambled eggs over the toasted bagel halves and serve with chilli jam.

TASTY PEPPER FRITTATA

This frittata makes a great little lunch or a light dinner. It can also be eaten cool, making it perfect for picnics – it's really convenient if cut into ready-to-eat slices.

SERVES 4
VEGETARIAN

1 TBSP OLIVE OIL

1 RED ONION, PEELED AND THINLY SLICED

2 LARGE RED PEPPERS, SLICED

2 GARLIC CLOVES, PEELED AND FINELY CHOPPED

8 LARGE EGGS

60ML (2¹/₂FL OZ) MILK

SEA SALT AND FRESHLY GROUND BLACK PEPPER

A SMALL HANDFUL OF FRESH BASIL, ROUGHLY CHOPPED

A KNOB OF BUTTER

- Preheat the grill to medium.

- Heat the oil in a large ovenproof frying pan (one that doesn't have a plastic handle) over a high heat, add the onion, peppers and garlic and fry for 3–4 minutes until tender.

- In a large bowl, whisk the eggs and milk together then season with a generous pinch of salt and black pepper. Add the cooked onion and pepper mixture and the fresh basil and stir to combine.

- Melt the knob of butter in the frying pan and pour in the egg mixture. Cook gently until the mixture sets but is still a little runny in the centre. Place the pan under the hot grill and cook until the egg on top is golden and bubbling.

- Serve in big chunky slices.

HUEVOS RANCHEROS

Fancy a breakfast with the heat turned up? These Mexican eggs pack a punch and will most definitely kick-start your day.

SERVES 2
VEGETARIAN

2 TBSP OLIVE OIL

1 ONION, PEELED AND FINELY CHOPPED

3 GARLIC CLOVES, PEELED AND FINELY CHOPPED

1 X 400G TIN OF CHOPPED TOMATOES

4 RED JALAPEÑO PEPPERS, ROUGHLY CHOPPED

1 TSP CHILLI POWDER, PLUS EXTRA TO SERVE (OPTIONAL)

4 WHOLEMEAL TORTILLA WRAPS

4 LARGE EGGS

A GOOD HANDFUL OF FRESH CORIANDER, ROUGHLY CHOPPED

50G (2OZ) FETA CHEESE, TO CRUMBLE

° Heat 1 tablespoon of olive oil in a large frying pan over a high heat. Add the onion and garlic and fry for 3–4 minutes until tender. Add the tomatoes, jalapeño peppers and chilli powder and simmer for 10–15 minutes until the sauce has thickened.

° Meanwhile, in another frying pan heat the tortilla wraps one at a time on both sides, or microwave according to the packet instructions. Remove and wrap in foil to keep warm.

° Add the remaining olive oil to the pan and crack the eggs in one at a time. Cook until the whites are set but the yolks are still a little soft. Place the eggs on the tortillas and top with the tomato salsa, a little chopped coriander, a dusting of chilli powder if you like and some feta cheese.

MEAT MARINADES

These marinades are super with any meat. I sometimes mix the
marinade in a resealable plastic bag, then drop in the meat, seal up
the bag, give it all a good squish, and pop in the fridge or freezer until
I'm ready to use it. Most meat will be good in the fridge for three days
or in the freezer for up to three months, still sitting in the marinade.
To make any of these marinades, simply mix all of the ingredients
until combined. Again, all the ingredients and quantities here are just
a starting point, so feel free to adapt them as you go.

BARBECUE

3 GARLIC CLOVES, PEELED AND FINELY CHOPPED

2 DASHES OF TABASCO SAUCE

1 TBSP WORCESTERSHIRE SAUCE

1 TBSP OLIVE OIL

1 TBSP SOFT DARK BROWN SUGAR

2 TBSP TOMATO KETCHUP

JUICE OF 1/2 LEMON

4–5 FRESH ROSEMARY SPRIGS, FINELY CHOPPED

1/2 TSP PAPRIKA

A GENEROUS PINCH OF SEA SALT AND FRESHLY GROUND BLACK PEPPER

GARLIC AND HERB

4 GARLIC CLOVES, PEELED AND CRUSHED

A FEW FRESH ROSEMARY SPRIGS, ROUGHLY CHOPPED

A FEW FRESH THYME SPRIGS, ROUGHLY CHOPPED

2 TBSP OLIVE OIL

JUICE OF 1 LEMON

A GOOD PINCH OF SEA SALT AND FRESHLY GROUND BLACK PEPPER

TERIYAKI

6 TBSP SOY SAUCE

2 TBSP CHINESE RICE WINE

1 THUMB-SIZED PIECE OF FRESH ROOT GINGER, PEELED AND FINELY CHOPPED

1 RED CHILLI, FINELY CHOPPED

3 GARLIC CLOVES, PEELED AND FINELY CHOPPED

2 TBSP HONEY

1 TBSP SUNFLOWER OIL

BALSAMIC

6 TBSP BALSAMIC VINEGAR

1 TBSP OLIVE OIL

1 TSP DIJON MUSTARD

3 GARLIC CLOVES, PEELED AND FINELY CHOPPED

1 TBSP SOFT DARK BROWN SUGAR

A GOOD PINCH OF SEA SALT AND FRESHLY GROUND BLACK PEPPER

ON TOAST

Lots of ingredients taste brilliant on toast, making a great little snack to keep you going. Here are some of my favourite toast toppings.

Basil and Mozzarella

There is nothing simpler or more satisfying to me than the combination of fresh basil, tomato and mozzarella on toast – a perfect little snack!

SERVES 2 GENEROUSLY
VEGETARIAN

2 LARGE VINE TOMATOES, CUT INTO CHUNKY SLICES

A FEW FRESH BASIL LEAVES

1 X 125G BALL OF GOOD-QUALITY MOZZARELLA CHEESE, TORN

SEA SALT AND FRESHLY GROUND BLACK PEPPER

EXTRA VIRGIN OLIVE OIL, FOR DRIZZLING

- Layer the toast with the tomato slices and roughly torn pieces of mozzarella. Scatter over the basil leaves then season with a generous pinch of salt and black pepper and a good drizzle of olive oil.

Garlic Mushrooms

You can't beat garlic mushrooms. If you are a garlic-fiend like I am, why not double the amount of garlic here?

SERVES 2 GENEROUSLY
VEGETARIAN

A GOOD KNOB OF BUTTER

1 TBSP OLIVE OIL

2 GARLIC CLOVES, PEELED AND FINELY CHOPPED

250G (9OZ) MUSHROOMS, SLICED

SEA SALT AND FRESHLY GROUND BLACK PEPPER

A GOOD HANDFUL OF FLAT LEAF PARSLEY, ROUGHLY CHOPPED, TO SERVE

- Heat the butter and olive oil in a large frying pan over a medium heat, add the garlic and fry for 30–40 seconds. Toss in the mushrooms and fry for 3–4 minutes until soft and tender. Season with a generous pinch of salt and black pepper and use the cooked mushrooms to top your toast, sprinkling with chopped parsley.

Proper Beans on Toast

For some, beans on toast is a bit of an art form, so I hope this version doesn't upset too many people. Creating your own makes all the difference and leaves you feeling full. You can also use haricot or borlotti beans. For a fully vegetarian dish, substitute with vegetarian Worcestershire sauce.

SERVES 2 GENEROUSLY

1 TBSP OLIVE OIL

2 GARLIC CLOVES, PEELED AND FINELY CHOPPED

½ RED ONION, PEELED AND FINELY SLICED

1 X 400G TIN OF CHOPPED TOMATOES

50ML (2FL OZ) RED WINE

1 TBSP WORCESTERSHIRE SAUCE

½ TSP GRANULATED SUGAR

SEA SALT AND FRESHLY GROUND BLACK PEPPER

1 X 400G TIN OF CANNELLINI BEANS, DRAINED AND RINSED

○ Heat the olive oil in a large frying pan over a medium heat, add the garlic and onion and fry for 4–5 minutes until soft. Add the chopped tomatoes, red wine, Worcestershire sauce and sugar. Bring to the boil then reduce the heat and simmer for 10 minutes until you have a thick sauce. Season with a generous pinch of salt and black pepper.

○ Add the cannellini beans to the pan and simmer for a further 5 minutes. Place generous spoonfuls onto the toast and enjoy.

Antipasto

This classic combination of ingredients makes a truly beautiful little snack or can even be enjoyed for breakfast.

SERVES 2 GENEROUSLY

2 SLICES OF PARMA HAM

A GOOD HANDFUL OF PARMESAN CHEESE SHAVINGS (ABOUT 50G/2OZ)

8 GREEN OLIVES, PITTED

250G (9OZ) SLOW-ROASTED CHERRY TOMATOES (SEE PAGE 77)

EXTRA VIRGIN OLIVE OIL, FOR DRIZZLING

○ Assemble the ham, cheese, olives and tomatoes on the toast and drizzle generously with olive oil.

MAYO

Homemade mayonnaise truly is something that you have to make yourself just to see how easy it actually is. The base of any good mayonnaise is decent ingredients, so get your hands on some fresh eggs and a good-quality olive oil. The beauty of making your own mayo means that you can tweak it with whatever flavours you desire. Here are just some of my favourites. Store in a jar in the fridge and use within 3–4 days.

Classic Mayo

SERVES 4
VEGETARIAN

1 EGG YOLK

½ TSP DIJON MUSTARD

2 TSP WHITE WINE VINEGAR

A PINCH OF SEA SALT

100ML (4FL OZ) SUNFLOWER OIL

2 TBSP EXTRA VIRGIN OLIVE OIL

- Place the egg yolk, mustard, vinegar and salt in a clean bowl.

- Pour the oils into a measuring jug that is easy to pour from. Steady the bowl by placing it on a damp tea towel as both hands will be occupied. With a large whisk in one hand and the jug of oil in the other, start to whisk the contents of the bowl, adding the oil drop by drop to start with. Be careful not to add too much oil too quickly as this may result in the mixture splitting. You can increase the oil to a thin stream once the mayonnaise starts to thicken. Be patient!

- Keep whisking until you have added all the oil and the mayonnaise is thick.

Perfect Aïoli

Add two peeled and crushed garlic cloves to the egg yolk at the start of the classic recipe and when the mayo is thick, mix through a small handful of chopped fresh flat-leaf parsley.

Herby Mayo

When the mayo is made, mix through a handful of chopped fresh mixed herbs (parsley, chives, basil, tarragon, mint, etc. – the choice is yours).

Curry Mayo

Stir a teaspoon of medium curry powder into the classic recipe and serve with crudités for a simple party starter.

Mince

Mince is a great stand-by ingredient as it freezes well and can be pulled out whenever you need it. Here are just a few of my favourite ways to use it.

SUPER BOLOGNESE

A good bolognese sauce was one of the first things I learned to cook, and it's a staple of many people's diets. This five-veg version is perfect for parents trying to sneak those extra veggies into their kids' meals. The addition of all the extra veg really pumps up the flavour. If you want to cut down on prep time, just blitz them in a food processor.

SERVES 4-6

2 TBSP OLIVE OIL

500G (1LB 2OZ) BEEF MINCE

1 ONION, PEELED AND FINELY CHOPPED

2 GARLIC CLOVES, PEELED AND FINELY CHOPPED

1 RED PEPPER, FINELY CHOPPED

1 SMALL CARROT, PEELED AND FINELY CHOPPED

1 SMALL COURGETTE, FINELY CHOPPED

75G (3OZ) CHESTNUT OR BUTTON MUSHROOMS, FINELY CHOPPED

1 X 400G TIN OF CHOPPED TOMATOES

100ML (4FL OZ) RED WINE

1 TSP DRIED OREGANO

SEA SALT AND FRESHLY GROUND BLACK PEPPER

A GOOD HANDFUL OF FRESH BASIL, ROUGHLY CHOPPED, PLUS EXTRA TO SERVE

- Heat 1 tablespoon of olive oil in a large frying pan over a high heat, add the minced beef and fry for 2–3 minutes until browned. Remove the mince from the pan and set aside on a plate.

- Heat the rest of the oil in the frying pan over a medium heat, add the onion and garlic and fry for 30–40 seconds. Add the pepper, carrot, courgette and mushrooms and fry for 4–5 minutes until tender. Return the minced beef to the pan with the chopped tomatoes, red wine and oregano, and season with salt and black pepper. Bring the sauce to the boil then reduce the heat and simmer gently for 15 minutes. Stir through the chopped basil.

- Serve with your choice of pasta or spaghetti, sprinkled with extra basil leaves, or use the sauce as required in other recipes. Store for up to 3–4 days in the fridge or 3 months in the freezer.

MINI AMERICAN MEAT LOAVES

These mini meat loaves go down really well with kids. If you're stuck for breadcrumbs, smash up some cream crackers – they're a perfect substitute.

SERVES 6

1 TBSP OLIVE OIL

2 LARGE ONIONS, PEELED AND FINELY CHOPPED

1 TSP DRIED OREGANO

SEA SALT AND FRESHLY GROUND BLACK PEPPER

1KG (2¼LB) BEEF MINCE

2 TBSP WORCESTERSHIRE SAUCE

½ TSP TABASCO SAUCE

75G (3OZ) FRESH WHITE BREADCRUMBS

1 LARGE EGG, BEATEN

100ML (4FL OZ) TOMATO KETCHUP (ABOUT 8 TBSP)

GREEN SALAD, TO SERVE

- Preheat the oven to 190°C (375°F), Gas mark 5.

- Heat the olive oil in a large frying pan over a medium heat, add the onions and oregano then season with a good pinch of salt and black pepper and cook gently, stirring every now and then, for 10 minutes until the onions are soft.

- Put the minced beef with the Worcestershire sauce, Tabasco, breadcrumbs, egg, a tablespoon of ketchup and the softened onions into a large bowl and, using your hands, mix until everything is combined.

- Divide the mixture into equal-sized loaf-shaped patties and place on a baking sheet. Spoon the remaining ketchup over the top of each meat loaf and bake in the oven for 35–40 minutes until they are cooked all the way through.

- Serve with a tasty green side salad.

EASY LASAGNE

Lasagne is always a crowd-pleaser and super easy to throw together if you have a batch of prepared bolognese, like the recipe on page 174. Simply make the cheese sauce, layer up the ingredients and then pop in the oven until golden on top . . . DELISH!

SERVES 4–6

1 QUANTITY OF SUPER BOLOGNESE (SEE PAGE 174)

4 SHEETS OF READY-TO-COOK LASAGNE

CHEESE SAUCE

50G (2OZ) BUTTER

50G (2OZ) PLAIN FLOUR

300ML (10¹/₂FL OZ) WARM MILK

150G (5OZ) CHEDDAR CHEESE, GRATED, PLUS EXTRA FOR SPRINKLING

1 TSP ENGLISH MUSTARD

SEA SALT AND FRESHLY GROUND BLACK PEPPER

○ Preheat the oven to 190°C (375°F), Gas mark 5.

○ To make the cheese sauce, melt the butter in a saucepan and stir in the flour quickly so you have a smooth paste. Gradually whisk in the warm milk and bring to the boil. Reduce the heat to a steady simmer and cook for 2 minutes until the sauce thickens. Remove the pan from the heat and add the cheese and mustard. Season with salt and black pepper.

○ Spoon half the bolognese into a high-sided baking dish then top with a third of the cheese sauce and two sheets of lasagne. Repeat the process, finishing with the final two sheets of lasagne, then cover with the remaining cheese sauce and sprinkle with extra grated cheese.

○ Bake in the oven for 25 minutes until bubbling and browned on top.

BANG IT IN THE OVEN SHEPHERD'S PIE

This is a great family favourite, which is super on cold winter evenings. It also freezes really well.

SERVES 4-6

1 QUANTITY OF SUPER BOLOGNESE SAUCE MADE USING LAMB MINCE (SEE PAGE 174)

1KG (2¼LB) POTATOES (PREFERABLY ROOSTERS), PEELED AND CUT INTO CUBES

3 TBSP BUTTER

2 LARGE EGG YOLKS

25G (1OZ) PARMESAN CHEESE, GRATED, PLUS EXTRA FOR SPRINKLING

SEA SALT AND FRESHLY GROUND BLACK PEPPER

- Preheat the oven to 190°C (375°F), Gas mark 5.

- Place the potatoes in a large saucepan of cold water and bring to the boil over a high heat. Reduce the heat to a simmer and cook for 12 minutes until tender when pierced with a fork. Drain, return the potatoes to the pan and mash until smooth. Beat in the butter and egg yolks and then stir through the grated Parmesan cheese.

- Spread the batch of bolognese sauce in the bottom of a high-sided baking dish and top with the mashed potato. Sprinkle a little extra Parmesan on top and season with salt and black pepper. Bake in the oven for 15–20 minutes until golden on top.

SALAD DRESSINGS

Incredibly easy, giving maximum taste, these will have you wondering why you didn't make your own salad dressings before. For each dressing, simply whisk the ingredients together, or to make them ahead of time, pop the ingredients in a clean jar, screw on the lid and shake well to combine. Feel free to experiment with the flavours, but stick to the golden rule of one part acidity (i.e. lemon or vinegar) to three parts oil, which helps give a balanced taste. Always dress salad at the very last minute or the leaves tend to wilt; you want them at their freshest and brightest. Keep the dressings in the fridge and use within 3–4 days.

ASIAN DRESSING

SERVES 4–6
VEGETARIAN

3 TBSP SUNFLOWER OIL

1 TBSP DARK SOY SAUCE

2 GARLIC CLOVES, PEELED
  AND FINELY CHOPPED

1 THUMB-SIZED PIECE OF FRESH ROOT
  GINGER, PEELED AND FINELY CHOPPED

2 TSP HONEY

JUICE OF 1 LIME

FRENCH MUSTARD DRESSING

SERVES 4–6
VEGETARIAN

1 GARLIC CLOVE, PEELED
  AND FINELY CHOPPED

1 TSP DIJON MUSTARD

1 TBSP WHITE WINE VINEGAR

1 TBSP LEMON JUICE

3 TBSP EXTRA VIRGIN OLIVE OIL

A GENEROUS PINCH OF SEA SALT
  AND FRESHLY GROUND BLACK PEPPER

CREAMY CHIVE DRESSING

SERVES 4–6
VEGETARIAN

3 TBSP EXTRA VIRGIN OLIVE OIL

1 TBSP CRÈME FRAÎCHE

JUICE OF 1/2 LEMON

A GENEROUS PINCH OF SEA SALT
  AND FRESHLY GROUND BLACK PEPPER

A GOOD HANDFUL OF CHIVES,
  FINELY CHOPPED

HERBY BALSAMIC DRESSING

SERVES 4–6
VEGETARIAN

1 GARLIC CLOVE, PEELED
  AND FINELY CHOPPED

A GOOD HANDFUL EACH OF FRESH
  ROSEMARY, THYME AND BASIL, FINELY
  CHOPPED, PLUS A COUPLE OF LARGE
  ROSEMARY SPRIGS

1 TSP HONEY

1 TBSP BALSAMIC VINEGAR

3 TBSP EXTRA VIRGIN OLIVE OIL

A GENEROUS PINCH OF SEA SALT AND
  FRESHLY GROUND BLACK PEPPER

RICE DISHES

Rice is an inexpensive staple store-cupboard ingredient that has so much more potential than just as a plain old side dish. Experiment with different types of rice – you should find a wide selection in your local supermarket. There are many varieties, so do try and think outside the box. Be careful when using leftover cooked rice – keep it in the fridge and use within 1 day.

Veggie Brown Rice Salad

Leftovers always make a great lunch and this is one of my favourite ways to use up leftover rice. Prep the ingredients and pop them in a lunch box; it couldn't be easier.

SERVES 4
VEGETARIAN

250G (9OZ) BROWN BASMATI RICE

1 GARLIC CLOVE, PEELED AND FINELY CHOPPED

3 TBSP EXTRA VIRGIN OLIVE OIL

1 TBSP BALSAMIC VINEGAR

1 X 400G TIN CHICKPEAS, DRAINED AND ROUGHLY CHOPPED

6 RAW OR BLANCHED ASPARAGUS SPEARS, FINELY CHOPPED

A GOOD HANDFUL OF FRESH FLAT LEAF PARSLEY, ROUGHLY CHOPPED

50G (2OZ) ROCKET LEAVES, ROUGHLY CHOPPED

SEA SALT AND FRESHLY GROUND BLACK PEPPER

- Use leftover cooked rice or prepare the rice according to the instructions on the packet, then drain and allow to cool.

- In a large bowl, whisk together the garlic, olive oil and balsamic vinegar. Add the cooked rice, chickpeas, asparagus spears, parsley and rocket and mix until everything is evenly combined. Season with salt and black pepper.

Aromatic Thai Rice

The rice in this dish takes on lots of beautiful, light flavours.

SERVES 4

250G (9OZ) BROWN BASMATI RICE

1 TBSP SUNFLOWER OIL

1 STALK LEMONGRASS

1 THUMB-SIZED PIECE OF FRESH ROOT GINGER, PEELED AND FINELY CHOPPED

6 SPRING ONIONS, FINELY SLICED

2 RED PEPPERS, FINELY DICED

1 TBSP FISH SAUCE (NAM PLA)

1 TBSP SOY SAUCE

JUICE OF 1 LIME

A GOOD HANDFUL OF FRESH CORIANDER LEAVES, ROUGHLY CHOPPED

○ Cook the rice according to the instructions on the packet then drain and allow to cool.

○ Meanwhile, heat the sunflower oil in a frying pan over a low-medium heat, add the lemongrass, ginger, spring onions and red peppers and gently fry until softened. Add the fish sauce, soy sauce and lime juice to season.

○ Spoon the rice into the pan and toss until all the flavours are combined and the rice is heated through then stir in the chopped coriander.

○ Serve as a pumped-up super side dish.

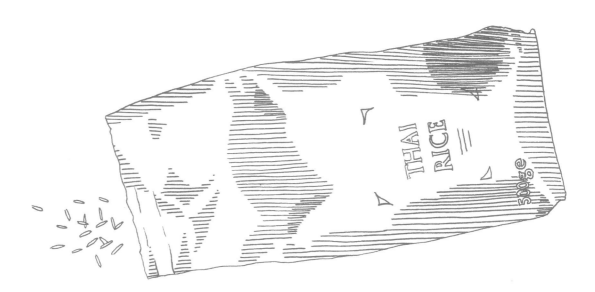

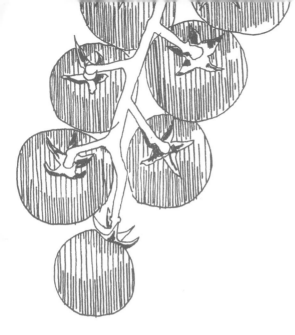

Stuffed Tomatoes with Rice

These stuffed tomatoes make a really substantial side dish.

SERVES 4

250G (9OZ) BROWN BASMATI RICE

4 LARGE TOMATOES

2 TBSP PESTO (SEE PAGE 155)

50G (2OZ) PINE NUTS

A GOOD HANDFUL OF FRESH BASIL,
ROUGHLY CHOPPED

2 TBSP OLIVE OIL

SEA SALT AND FRESHLY
GROUND BLACK PEPPER

- Cook the rice according to the instructions on the packet then drain and allow to cool.

- Preheat the oven to 180°C (350°F), Gas mark 4.

- Cut the tops off the tomatoes (reserving the tops), then scoop out the insides and place the flesh in a bowl. Add the cooled rice, pesto and pine nuts and stir through the basil. Place the scooped-out tomatoes in a roasting tray and drizzle with the olive oil. Season with salt and black pepper.

- Fill each tomato with some of the rice mix and cover with one of the tomato tops. Bake in the oven for 25 minutes. Serve with meat or fish dishes.

Squash and Crispy Pancetta Risotto

I absolutely love this recipe – it is a really cosy dish, leaving you full, satisfied and warm. Risotto may seem a little tricky, but it's just a case of keeping an eye on it and slowly incorporating the liquid, so give it a go. If you can't get your hands on pancetta slices, use smoked streaky bacon instead.

SERVES 4

850G (1LB 13OZ) BUTTERNUT SQUASH, PEELED, SLICED IN HALF AND CUT LENGTHWAYS INTO SLICES

3 GARLIC CLOVES, PEELED AND ROUGHLY SLICED

A FEW FRESH THYME SPRIGS

SEA SALT AND FRESHLY GROUND BLACK PEPPER

4 TBSP OLIVE OIL

8 SLICES OF PANCETTA

1 LITRE (1¾ PINTS) CHICKEN STOCK

150G (5OZ) BUTTER

1 ONION, PEELED AND FINELY CHOPPED

300G (11OZ) RISOTTO RICE

75ML (3FL OZ) WHITE WINE

150G (5OZ) PARMESAN CHEESE, GRATED

- Preheat the oven to 220°C (425°F), Gas mark 7. Place the squash on a roasting tray with the garlic, thyme, a good pinch of salt and black pepper and half the olive oil and toss together.

- Cover with foil and bake in the oven for 50 minutes until the squash is soft. Ten minutes before the squash is ready, remove the foil, lay the pancetta over the squash and continue to bake until the pancetta is crisp. When the pumpkin and pancetta are cooked, remove the tray from the oven, take the pancetta off the pumpkin and set both aside.

- Pour the stock into a saucepan and simmer gently.

- Heat 75g (3oz) of the butter and the remaining olive oil in a large frying pan, add the onion and fry over a low-medium heat for about 10 minutes until soft. Add the rice and stir until it is coated in the butter and oil.

- Pour in the white wine, bring to the boil and let it bubble until nearly evaporated, then start adding the warm stock, about two ladlefuls at a time, allowing it to be absorbed before adding more. Continue to add the stock until the rice is tender and has a creamy coating. This should take about 15 minutes.

- Add the remaining butter, the roasted squash and garlic and the grated Parmesan and gently stir though. Season to taste with salt and black pepper. Serve immediately with the crispy slices of pancetta on top.

EASY DESSERTS & BAKING

In my opinion, if you're going to take the time to make a dessert, then you ought to go all-out and create a dessert that will make people go 'Wow!' Even though you may have already impressed your guests by cooking an amazing main course, why not take it that one step further and pull something sweet out of the oven or fridge? It will have them singing your praises for weeks after! If you can master a few of these easy desserts, you can then prepare them at the drop of a hat without too much trouble. Some of the first sweet dishes I ever learned to cook were baked in the oven. For young cooks, the whole process of measuring, sifting, mixing, stirring and scooping makes for fantastic entertainment, so it's what I spent a lot of my time as a kid doing. It really is a wonderful way of getting children involved and you'll soon have a few little kitchen heroes in the making.

BLUEBERRY AND LEMON SCONES

Adding different flavours to plain old scones really rocks up the flavours. I promise there is nothing better than warm scones straight out of the oven with just a little butter – DELICIOUS! The scones also freeze quite well.

MAKES 10-12 SCONES

250G (9OZ) PLAIN FLOUR,
   PLUS EXTRA FOR DUSTING

1 TBSP BAKING POWDER

1 TSP SALT

40G (1½OZ) COLD BUTTER,
   CUT INTO SMALL PIECES

45G (1½OZ) CASTER SUGAR

2-3 TBSP BUTTERMILK,
   PLUS EXTRA FOR BRUSHING

1 LARGE EGG, BEATEN

100G (3½OZ) BLUEBERRIES

FINELY GRATED ZEST OF 1 LEMON

EQUIPMENT

A 6CM (2½IN) DIAMETER PASTRY
   CUTTER OR GLASS

- Preheat the oven to 200°C (400°F), Gas mark 6 and dust a baking sheet generously with flour.

- Sift the flour, baking powder and salt into a large bowl. Add the butter and, using your fingertips, rub it into the flour until the mixture resembles rough breadcrumbs. Stir in the caster sugar then add the buttermilk, egg, blueberries and lemon zest and, using a spoon, bring the dough together.

- Turn the dough out onto a floured work surface and roll into a 2.5cm (1in) thick round. Using the pastry cutter or a glass, cut out the scones and place on the prepared baking sheet. Re-roll the pastry, if necessary, to cut out the remaining scones.

- Brush the scones with a little extra buttermilk and bake in the oven for 10–15 minutes until risen and golden in colour.

- Remove the scones from the oven and place on a wire rack to cool, if you can wait that long!

EASY APPLE SLICES

Warm caramelised apples, crisp flaky pastry, tangy sweet juices and a light dusting of icing sugar . . . are you hungry yet? These apple slices make the most beautiful little dessert, which doesn't take too much time or effort to throw together. Don't worry about being overly careful when arranging the apples on the pastry. I like my apple slices to look homemade and a bit rough and ready.

SERVES 4

200G (7OZ) PLAIN FLOUR, SIFTED, PLUS EXTRA FOR DUSTING

1 TBSP CASTER SUGAR

150G (5OZ) BUTTER, CUT INTO SMALL PIECES

FILLING

3 LARGE COOKING APPLES, PEELED, CORED AND THINLY SLICED

75G (3OZ) SOFT DARK BROWN SUGAR

50G (2OZ) BUTTER, CUT INTO SMALL PIECES

TO SERVE

A LITTLE DUSTING OF ICING SUGAR

WHIPPED CREAM

- To make the pastry, place the flour and caster sugar in a large bowl. Add the butter and, using your fingertips, rub it into the flour and sugar until the mixture resembles rough breadcrumbs. Add 3 tablespoons of cold water, a little at a time, and bring the dough together to form a ball. Wrap the dough in cling film and place in the fridge to rest for at least 1 hour.

- Preheat the oven to 200°C (400°F), Gas mark 6 and line a baking sheet with baking parchment.

- Roll the pastry out on a lightly floured work surface to a 30 x 15cm (12 x 6in) rectangle and carefully transfer to the prepared baking sheet.

- Toss the apple pieces with the brown sugar in a bowl then arrange them on top of the pastry, leaving a gap of about 2.5cm (1in) all the way around the edge. Lift up the edge of the pastry and fold it in on itself towards the apples so that you have a raised border all the way around. Dot the apples with a little butter.

- Bake in the oven for 45 minutes until the apples are caramelised and the pastry is golden brown. Remove from the oven and allow to cool slightly before slicing into individual servings. Dust with icing sugar and serve with a little whipped cream.

Apple and Blackberry Pie

Homemade pies always remind me of those big juicy ones in the Tom and Jerry cartoons that would be left to cool on the windowsill, invariably setting the scene for havoc to ensue! This pie will get everyone just as excited.

SERVES 6-8

330G (12OZ) PLAIN FLOUR, PLUS EXTRA FOR DUSTING

PINCH OF SALT

175G (6OZ) COLD BUTTER, CUT INTO SMALL PIECES

1 LARGE EGG, LIGHTLY BEATEN

CREAM OR CUSTARD, TO SERVE

FILLING

750G (1LB 7OZ) COOKING APPLES, PEELED, CORED AND CUT INTO SMALL CHUNKS

750G (1LB 10OZ) BLACKBERRIES

100G (3½OZ) CASTER SUGAR, PLUS EXTRA FOR SPRINKLING

JUICE OF ½ LEMON

1 TBSP PLAIN FLOUR

EQUIPMENT

A 23CM (9IN) TART TIN, ABOUT 2.5CM (1IN) DEEP, WITH A REMOVABLE BASE

○ To make the pastry, sift the flour and salt into a large bowl. Add the butter and, using your fingertips, rub it into the flour until the mixture resembles fine breadcrumbs. Add 4–6 tablespoons of water, a tablespoon at a time, and bring the dough together to form a ball. (You may not need all the water.) Wrap the dough in cling film and place in the fridge to rest for at least 15 minutes.

○ For the filling, toss the apples and blackberries together in a bowl with the sugar, lemon juice and flour.

○ Preheat the oven to 180°C (350°F), Gas mark 4.

○ Roll out two-thirds of the pastry on a lightly floured work surface to a 29cm (11½in) circle. Gently lift the dough with a rolling pin and transfer it to the tart tin. Press the pastry into the base and sides of the tin then trim the pastry level with the edges of the tart tin. Knead any scraps into the remaining dough. Spoon the apples and blackberries into the pastry case.

○ Roll out the remaining pastry on a lightly floured work surface to a 24cm (9½in) circle and cut the circle into 2.5cm (1in) wide strips. Brush the pastry rim with a little beaten egg then weave the strips over the berries in a lattice pattern, pressing the ends on to the pastry rim. Trim any excess pastry. Brush the lattice with more beaten egg and sprinkle with a little extra sugar.

○ Bake the pie in the oven for 45 minutes–1 hour until the pastry is golden and the juices are bubbling. Transfer to a wire rack and allow to cool. Serve hot with fresh cream or custard.

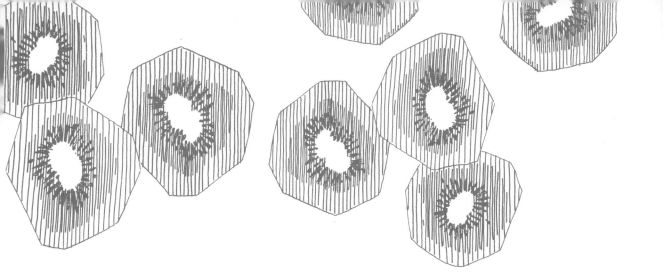

KIWI, RASPBERRY AND MINT FRUIT SALAD

This is good as a really fresh and zingy breakfast or a delicious light dessert. The combination of colours is fantastic and the flavours will wake up your taste buds. I make it with just kiwi and mint when fresh raspberries are out of season.

SERVES 4

6 KIWI FRUITS

125G (4½OZ) FRESH RASPBERRIES

3 LARGE FRESH MINT SPRIGS, CHOPPED

- Peel and slice the kiwi fruits into rounds, showing the bright centres. Arrange the slices on a serving plate, scatter over the raspberries and sprinkle the plate with the chopped mint – it couldn't be simpler!

Shortbread with Vanilla Sugar Strawberries

Come to think of it, shortbread may well be the first thing I learned to bake when I was growing up. My best buddy Jonathan and I used to sell it to the neighbours – I know, we were strange kids! This recipe makes a warm, crumbly, buttery biscuit which goes perfectly with the intense sweetness of fresh strawberries. If you can't get your hands on vanilla sugar, you can make your own very simply, by placing one or two vanilla pods in a jar of caster sugar. After a few days, you will end up with vanilla sugar.

SERVES 4

100G (3½OZ) COLD BUTTER, CUT INTO SMALL PIECES

150G (5OZ) PLAIN FLOUR, SIFTED, PLUS EXTRA FOR DUSTING

50G (2OZ) GRANULATED SUGAR

1 TSP VANILLA EXTRACT

250G (9OZ) FRESH STRAWBERRIES, HULLED AND HALVED

4 TBSP VANILLA SUGAR

WHIPPED CREAM, TO SERVE

- Place the flour in a large bowl, add the butter and, using your fingertips, rub it into the flour until the mixture resembles breadcrumbs. Stir through the sugar and vanilla extract and press into a dough. Wrap in cling film and place in the fridge to rest for 15 minutes.

- While the dough is resting, combine the strawberries with the vanilla sugar and set aside.

- Preheat the oven to 180°C (350°F), Gas mark 4.

- Roll out the dough on a floured work surface then cut out biscuit shapes (whatever shape you like) and place on a non-stick baking tray. Bake in the oven for 15–20 minutes or until pale golden brown.

- Remove the biscuits from the oven and allow to cool on a wire rack, then serve with the strawberries and a dollop of whipped cream.

BASIC CUPCAKES

These cupcakes are adapted from my Aunt Erica's fairy cake recipe. If you are making them for kids to decorate and you want to limit the time it takes to put everything together, it may be easier to make the cupcakes in advance and then get the kids to decorate them later on.

MAKES 8–10 CUPCAKES

175G (6OZ) SELF-RAISING FLOUR, SIFTED

110G (4OZ) CASTER SUGAR

1 TSP BAKING POWDER

2 LARGE EGGS

110G (4OZ) BUTTER OR SOFT MARGARINE, SOFTENED AND CUT INTO SMALL PIECES

50ML (2FL OZ) MILK OR WATER

FROSTING

150G (5OZ) BUTTER, SOFTENED AND CUT INTO SMALL PIECES

½ TSP VANILLA EXTRACT (OPTIONAL)

275G (10OZ) ICING SUGAR

TO DECORATE

FOOD COLOURING

SPRINKLES

EQUIPMENT

12-HOLE BUN TRAY

A PIPING BAG FITTED WITH A NOZZLE

- Preheat the oven to 180°C (350°F), Gas mark 4 and line the bun tray with 8–10 paper cases.

- In a large bowl, combine all the dry ingredients. Make a well in the centre of the bowl then break in the eggs and add the butter or margarine. Using an electric hand mixer, beat all the ingredients together until combined. Pour in half the milk or water and beat again until combined. You are looking for the batter to be light and creamy. Add the rest of the liquid if you need it – you may not.

- Divide the batter evenly among the paper cases and bake in the oven for 15–20 minutes until firm to the touch and light brown on top. Allow the cupcakes to stand for a minute before transferring to a wire rack to cool.

- To make the frosting, beat together the butter and vanilla extract (if using) in a bowl until light and fluffy then sift in the icing sugar, a little at a time, until it is incorporated and the mixture is smooth. At this point you can separate the frosting into different bowls and stir through food colourings if you wish.

- Spoon the frosting into the piping bag and ice away. Let your imagination go wild! Top with sprinkles or other decorations.

BURSTING BLUEBERRY CUPCAKES

These blueberry cupcakes, with their natural ingredients, are a great alternative to some of the more artificial flavours that cupcakes come in. To make blueberry purée, simple blitz a punnet of blueberries with a hand-held blender until smooth, or pop them in a food processor.

MAKES 8-10 CUPCAKES

4 TBSP BLUEBERRY PURÉE (SEE INTRO)

1 QUANTITY OF CUPCAKE MIXTURE (SEE PAGE 196)

BLUEBERRIES, TO DECORATE

FROSTING

225G (8OZ) FULL-FAT CREAM CHEESE, AT ROOM TEMPERATURE

375G (13OZ) ICING SUGAR

2 TBSP BLUEBERRY PURÉE

EQUIPMENT

12-HOLE BUN TRAY

A PIPING BAG FITTED WITH A NOZZLE

- Preheat the oven to 180°C (350°F), Gas mark 4 and line the bun tray with 8-10 paper cases.

- Stir the blueberry purée into the cupcake mixture until evenly incorporated.

- Divide the batter evenly among the paper cases and bake in the oven for 15–20 minutes until firm to the touch and light brown on top. Allow the cupcakes to stand for a minute before transferring to a wire rack to cool.

- For the frosting, beat the cream cheese in a bowl until soft then sift in the icing sugar, a little at a time, until it is incorporated and the mixture is smooth. Stir through the blueberry purée until combined.

- Spoon the frosting into the piping bag and ice away! Place 3-4 blueberries on top of each cupcake to decorate.

SWIT-SWOO CHOCOLATE HONEYCOMB CUPCAKES

Just when you thought cupcakes couldn't get sweeter . . . well, how about throwing some honeycomb in there too?

MAKES 8–10 CUPCAKES

1 TBSP COCOA POWDER, SIFTED

125G (4½OZ) HONEYCOMB, ROUGHLY CHOPPED, OR 3 CRUNCHIE BARS, CHOPPED INTO CHUNKS, PLUS EXTRA TO DECORATE

1 QUANTITY OF CUPCAKE MIXTURE (SEE PAGE 196)

FROSTING

150G (5OZ) BUTTER, SOFTENED AND CUT INTO SMALL PIECES

275G (10OZ) ICING SUGAR

1 TBSP COCOA POWDER

4 TBSP DULCE DE LECHE (CARAMELISED CONDENSED MILK)

EQUIPMENT

12-HOLE BUN TRAY

A PIPING BAG FITTED WITH A NOZZLE

- Preheat the oven to 180°C (350°F), Gas mark 4 and line the bun tray with 8–10 paper cases.

- Stir the cocoa powder and honeycomb into the cupcake mixture until evenly incorporated.

- Divide the batter evenly among the paper cases and bake in the oven for 15–20 minutes or until firm to the touch. Allow the cupcakes to stand for a minute before transferring to a wire rack to cool.

- For the frosting, beat the butter in a bowl until light and fluffy then sift in the icing sugar and cocoa powder, a little at a time, until fully incorporated and the mixture is smooth. Stir in the dulce de leche until evenly combined.

- Spoon the frosting into the piping bag and ice away! Sprinkle with a little extra roughly chopped honeycomb or Crunchie bar.

GOLDEN CHOCOLATE CHIP CUPCAKES

I love the texture of these cupcakes; the chocolate chips are a great contrast to the silky chocolate batter. If you can get your hands on edible gold powder, dust it over the top of the frosting to give an amazing golden sheen.

MAKES 8-10 CUPCAKES

2 TBSP COCOA POWDER, SIFTED

100G (3½OZ) CHOCOLATE CHIPS (WHITE, MILK OR PLAIN)

1 QUANTITY OF CUPCAKE MIXTURE (SEE PAGE 196)

EDIBLE GOLD POWDER, FOR DUSTING

FROSTING

110G (4OZ) BUTTER, SOFTENED AND CUT INTO SMALL PIECES

1 TSP VANILLA EXTRACT

325G (12OZ) ICING SUGAR

4 TBSP COCOA POWDER

75ML (3FL OZ) DOUBLE CREAM

EQUIPMENT

12-HOLE BUN TRAY

A PIPING BAG FITTED WITH A NOZZLE

- Preheat the oven to 180°C (350°F), Gas mark 4 and line the bun tray with 8-10 paper cases.

- Stir the cocoa powder and chocolate chips into the cupcake mixture until evenly incorporated.

- Divide the batter evenly among the paper cases and bake in the oven for 15–20 minutes or until firm to the touch. Allow the cupcakes to stand for a minute before transferring to a wire rack to cool.

- For the frosting, beat the butter and vanilla extract together in a bowl until light and fluffy then sift in the icing sugar and cocoa powder, a little at a time, until fully incorporated and the mixture is smooth. Stir in the cream until evenly combined.

- Spoon the frosting into the piping bag and ice away! Sift a little edible gold powder over the top for that extra touch.

STICKY TOFFEE CUPCAKES

This variation makes a wonderfully sticky and rich cupcake. Topping it with pecan nuts is simply a must!

MAKES 8–10 CUPCAKES

110G (4OZ) STONED DATES, FINELY CHOPPED

½ TSP BICARBONATE OF SODA

½ TSP VANILLA EXTRACT

1 TSP INSTANT COFFEE GRANULES

1 QUANTITY OF CUPCAKE MIXTURE (SEE PAGE 196)

FROSTING

110G (4OZ) BUTTER, SOFTENED AND CUT INTO SMALL PIECES

175G (6OZ) ICING SUGAR

4 TBSP DULCE DE LECHE (CARAMELISED CONDENSED MILK), PLUS A LITTLE EXTRA TO DRIZZLE OVER THE TOP

8–10 PECAN HALVES, TO DECORATE

EQUIPMENT

12-HOLE BUN TRAY

A PIPING BAG FITTED WITH A NOZZLE

- Preheat the oven to 180°C (350°F), Gas mark 4 and line the bun tray with 8–10 paper cases.

- Place the chopped dates in a bowl, add the bicarbonate of soda, vanilla extract and coffee and cover with 100ml (4fl oz) of boiling water. Allow to stand for 10–15 minutes to soften the dates.

- If there is any water left after the dates have softened and cooled, drain before folding them into the cupcake mixture. Divide the batter evenly among the paper cases and bake in the oven for 15–20 minutes until firm to the touch and light brown on top. Allow the cupcakes to stand for a minute before transferring to a wire rack to cool.

- For the frosting, beat the butter in a bowl until light and fluffy then add the icing sugar, a little at a time, until it is all incorporated and the mixture is smooth. Add the dulce de leche and stir through to combine.

- Spoon the frosting into the piping bag and ice away! Top with pecan halves and drizzle with a little extra dulce de leche.

Strawberry and Rhubarb Oaty Crumble

Crumble has to be one of the easiest desserts to prepare and it is extremely easy to adapt, using whatever fruit is in season. You can vary the ingredients for the crumble mix itself. I sometimes use wholemeal flour and nuts, though I'm a complete stickler for using jumbo oats as they give the dessert a really crunchy nutty texture.

SERVES 4

150G (5OZ) PLAIN FLOUR

150G (5OZ) JUMBO OAT FLAKES

175G (6OZ) SOFT LIGHT BROWN SUGAR

200G (7OZ) COLD BUTTER, CUT INTO SMALL PIECES

SINGLE CREAM, TO SERVE

FILLING

600G (1LB 4OZ) FRESH STRAWBERRIES, HULLED

5 MEDIUM STALKS OF RHUBARB, TRIMMED AND CUT INTO 2.5CM (1IN) PIECES

1 TBSP PLAIN FLOUR

60G (2½OZ) SOFT LIGHT BROWN SUGAR

JUICE OF ½ LEMON

- Preheat the oven to 190°C (375°F), Gas mark 5.

- Place the flour, oat flakes, brown sugar and butter in a large bowl. Using your fingertips, rub all the ingredients together until the mixture resembles chunky breadcrumbs.

- In a large baking dish, toss the strawberries and rhubarb with the flour, sugar and lemon juice until combined. Add the crumble mix and spread over the top of the filling until evenly covered.

- Bake in the oven for 35–40 minutes until the crumble topping is golden brown and the fruit is soft and bubbling beneath. Serve in generous portions with a drizzle of fresh cream.

FAT BOY'S PEANUT BUTTER SNICKER SQUARES

This recipe makes delicious squares, which are miles better and totally different from any bars you can buy in the shops – way more chewy, crunchy and chocolaty and totally worth it! I used 100g (3½oz) of white chocolate and 100g (3½oz) of milk chocolate for the ones in the photo and swirled the two together to get a super marbled effect.

MAKES ABOUT 20 SQUARES

200G (7OZ) GOOD-QUALITY CHOCOLATE, WHITE, MILK OR DARK DEPENDING ON YOUR PREFERENCE, BROKEN INTO PIECES

200G (7OZ) SMOOTH PEANUT BUTTER

100G (3½OZ) CASTER SUGAR

200ML (7FL OZ) GOLDEN SYRUP

100G (3½OZ) SPECIAL K FLAKES

100G (3½OZ) COCONUT FLAKES

EQUIPMENT

20CM (8IN) SQUARE DEEP BAKING TIN

○ Line the baking tin with baking parchment.

○ Put the chocolate in a heatproof bowl, set over a small saucepan of barely simmering water, making sure the base of the bowl does not touch the water, and allow to melt gently.

○ Melt the peanut butter, sugar and golden syrup together in another saucepan over a gentle heat until runny and smooth.

○ In a large bowl, toss the Special K flakes and flaked coconut until combined.

○ Pour the peanut butter mixture over the dry ingredients and, using a wooden spoon, stir until everything is nicely combined. Turn the mixture out into the baking tin and spread out evenly, pressing down with the back of a spoon.

○ Pour over the melted chocolate, again spreading evenly, and place in the fridge to chill for a few hours until firm. These are very sweet so I cut them into 4cm (1½in) squares.

MINI LEMON MERINGUE PIES

The lemon curd in this recipe would make a grown man weep for joy!
I just love the appearance of these mini pies – they look like a cupcake
mixed with a Mr Whippy ice cream. Totally delicious.

MAKES 18-20 MINI PIES

330G (12OZ) PLAIN FLOUR,
  PLUS EXTRA FOR DUSTING

PINCH OF SALT

3 TBSP CASTER SUGAR

175G (6OZ) COLD BUTTER, CUT
  INTO SMALL PIECES, PLUS EXTRA
  FOR GREASING

LEMON FILLING

300G (11OZ) CASTER SUGAR

100G (3½OZ) CORNFLOUR

120ML (4½FL OZ) LEMON JUICE
  (2-3 LEMONS)

4 LARGE EGG YOLKS

A PINCH OF SALT

FINELY GRATED ZEST OF 2 LEMONS

60G (2½OZ) BUTTER

MERINGUE

250G (9OZ) ICING SUGAR, SIFTED

4 LARGE EGG WHITES

EQUIPMENT

TWO 12-HOLE MUFFIN TRAYS

1 PIPING BAG FITTED WITH
  A 1CM (½IN) NOZZLE

○ To make the pastry, sift the flour and salt into a large bowl. Add the caster sugar and combine then add the butter and, using your fingertips, rub it into the flour until the mixture resembles fine breadcrumbs. Add 4-6 tablespoons of water, a tablespoon at a time, until the dough comes together to form a ball. Wrap the dough in cling film and place it in the fridge to rest for at least 15 minutes.

○ While the dough is resting, make the filling. Place the sugar, cornflour and 450ml (16fl oz) of water in a large saucepan and stir until you have a smooth mixture. Stir in the lemon juice, egg yolks and salt. Bring to the boil and keep stirring while the mixture boils, for 10-12 minutes. Stir in the lemon zest and butter, allowing the butter to melt, then remove the pan from the heat and allow to cool.

○ Preheat the oven to 180°C (350°F), Gas mark 4 and grease and flour the muffin trays. Roll out the pastry on a lightly floured work surface into a rectangle about 3mm (⅛in) thick. Cut 9cm (3½in) squares out of the pastry and place in the prepared muffin trays. Pierce the bottoms with a fork and place in the oven for 10 minutes. Remove from the oven and set aside to cool. Reduce the oven temperature to 170°C (325°F), Gas mark 3.

○ In a stand-alone mixer or using a hand-held electric mixer, whisk the icing sugar and egg whites together on high for 10 minutes until stiff glossy peaks form. Put the meringue mixture into the piping bag. Top each pastry case with a little of the lemon filling and cover with a generous Mr Whippy-style swirl of meringue. Bake on the middle shelf of the oven for 10-15 minutes until the edges are browned. Remove from the oven and allow to cool before taking a bite.

Blueberry and White Chocolate Cheesecake

This makes a wonderfully creamy and rich cheesecake. A perfect make-ahead dessert, it can be prepared in advance and popped in the fridge until needed.

SERVES 6-8

200G (7OZ) PLAIN DIGESTIVE BISCUITS

100G (3½OZ) BUTTER

400G (14OZ) GOOD-QUALITY WHITE CHOCOLATE, BROKEN INTO PIECES

250G (9OZ) FULL-FAT CREAM CHEESE

250ML (8½FL OZ) DOUBLE CREAM

250G (9OZ) MASCARPONE CHEESE

250G (9OZ) BLUEBERRIES

EQUIPMENT

A 20CM (8IN) NON-STICK SPRINGFORM CAKE TIN

- Bash the biscuits in a resealable bag with a rolling pin, or any other blunt instrument you can do serious damage with, until you have fine crumbs.

- Melt the butter in a large saucepan then add the biscuit crumbs and mix to combine. Tip the butter and biscuit mix into the base of the springform tin and press down with the back of a spoon. Cover and place in the fridge to chill while you prepare the rest of the ingredients.

- Place the chocolate in a heatproof bowl then set it over a small saucepan of barely simmering water, making sure the base of the bowl does not touch the water, and gently melt, stirring occasionally.

- Beat the cream cheese, cream and mascarpone in a large bowl with a wooden spoon until well combined. Stir through the white chocolate and lastly fold in the blueberries. Spread the mixture evenly over the top of the biscuit base, then cover and place in the fridge to chill and set for at least 2-3 hours.

- Remove the cheesecake from the tin and serve in generous slices.

Chocolate Chip Cookies

The best way to get nice even cookies is to use a medium-sized ice cream scoop. This will not only give you professional-looking cookies, but also totally simplify the spooning-out process. If you can't get your hands on chocolate chips, just break up some good-quality chocolate bars and that will do the trick.

MAKES 8-10 COOKIES

225G (8OZ) BUTTER, SOFTENED, PLUS EXTRA FOR GREASING (OPTIONAL)

140G (5OZ) SOFT DARK BROWN SUGAR

140G (5OZ) GRANULATED SUGAR

A PINCH OF SALT

1 TSP VANILLA EXTRACT

1 LARGE EGG

240G (8½OZ) PLAIN FLOUR, SIFTED

300G (11OZ) MILK CHOCOLATE CHIPS

- Preheat the oven to 190°C (375°F), Gas mark 5. Grease two large baking trays or line with baking parchment.

- Beat the sugars, salt, vanilla extract and butter together in a large bowl with a wooden spoon until smooth. Add the egg and beat again, until thoroughly mixed. Mix in the flour and when the dough begins to form, add the chocolate chips and mix again lightly, until everything is combined.

- Using a medium-sized ice cream scoop or a large tablespoon, spoon the dough onto the prepared baking trays, leaving about 5cm (2in) between each, as the cookies will spread out as they cook.

- Bake in the oven for 10–12 minutes until the edges of the cookies are golden brown and the middle still slightly pale. Allow to set a little in the trays, then transfer to a wire rack to cool. Enjoy the cookies old-school style: a little warm with a nice cool glass of milk.

SUPER CHOCOLATE BROWNIES

I have done my market research on this recipe and can safely say that both kids and adults will go wild for these deadly chocolate brownies. My one piece of advice is to make a double batch as they won't last long. Wrapped up, in a nice box, they also make great presents.

MAKES 24 BROWNIES

225G (8OZ) GOOD-QUALITY DARK CHOCOLATE, BROKEN INTO PIECES

225G (8OZ) BUTTER

300G (11OZ) CASTER SUGAR

3 LARGE EGGS, BEATEN

1 TSP VANILLA EXTRACT

75G (3OZ) PLAIN FLOUR

1 TSP BAKING POWDER

EQUIPMENT

A 22 X 30CM (9 X 12IN) BAKING TIN

- Preheat the oven to 180°C (350°F), Gas mark 4. Line the baking tin with baking parchment.

- Place the chocolate and butter in a heatproof bowl and set over a saucepan of barely simmering water, making sure the base of the bowl does not touch the water. Stir constantly until melted and smooth.

- With a hand-held electric mixer, whisk the sugar and eggs together for 2–3 minutes until pale and fluffy. Slowly add the melted chocolate and butter then add the vanilla extract and continue to whisk until thickened. Lastly, sift in the flour and baking powder and fold in gently.

- Turn the mixture into the prepared tin and bake in the middle shelf of the oven for 30 minutes until the top is firm and the cake has come away slightly from the sides of the tin. Remove from the oven and allow to cool in the tin. When cooled cut into 24 squares. You'd be welcome at anyone's house with these!

WHOOPIE PIES

During my search for the perfect whoopie pie, I was sent this recipe by a reader of my blog, whose mother-in-law, Mrs Linda Daunt, has lived all her life in Maine, New England, and is a fantastic cook. She bakes these pies for special occasions: Christmas, Easter, Thanksgiving, birthdays, weddings, funerals, and occasionally by special request when one of her daughters feels nostalgic for her childhood. Mrs Daunt's special touch is to add buttermilk instead of regular milk, to give the pies a richer taste. The original recipe uses a marshmallow-type filling, but I prefer to stick with regular buttercream frostings. See overleaf for more filling varieties.

MAKES 16 WHOOPIE PIES

270G (10OZ) PLAIN FLOUR

5 TBSP GOOD-QUALITY COCOA POWDER

1 TSP BAKING POWDER

A PINCH OF SALT

190G (6½OZ) CASTER SUGAR

120G (4½OZ) BUTTER, SOFTENED

2 LARGE EGGS, LIGHTLY BEATEN

1 TSP VANILLA EXTRACT

250ML (8½FL OZ) BUTTERMILK

FILLING

150G (5OZ) BUTTER, SOFTENED

½ TSP VANILLA EXTRACT

275G (10OZ) ICING SUGAR, SIFTED

- Preheat the oven to 180°C (350°F), Gas mark 4 and line two baking sheets with baking parchment.

- Sift the flour, cocoa powder, baking powder and salt into a bowl. In another bowl, using a hand-held electric mixer, cream the sugar and the butter until pale and fluffy. Gradually add the eggs, mixing well to combine.

- Add the vanilla extract to the buttermilk and, alternating with the dry ingredients, add to the creamed butter mixture, mixing until everything is combined and you have a thick batter. Spoon 32 rounded teaspoons of the batter onto the prepared baking sheets, allowing about 5cm (2in) of space for them to spread while cooking. Bake in the oven for about 15 minutes until the tops have puffed up and spring back when lightly pressed.

- While the pie halves are baking, prepare the filling by beating the butter in a bowl until pale and creamy. Add the vanilla extract and gradually add the icing sugar until the mixture is light and fluffy.

- When the pie halves are cooked, leave them on the baking sheets for 5 minutes then remove with a metal spatula and place on a wire rack to cool. Once cooled, spread a rounded teaspoon of the creamy filling on the flat side of one pie half and sandwich together with another. Et voilà, whoopie pies!

MINT CHOCOLATE WHOOPIES

Follow the original whoopie recipe but sandwich the pie halves together with this minty green frosting. This is my favourite whoopie variety.

MAKES 16 WHOOPIE PIES

1 X QUANTITY OF BASIC WHOOPIE PIE MIXTURE (SEE PAGE 213)

FILLING

150G (5OZ) BUTTER, SOFTENED

275G (10OZ) ICING SUGAR, SIFTED

¼ TSP PEPPERMINT EXTRACT

½ TSP GREEN FOOD COLOURING (OPTIONAL)

- Spoon the whoopie pie mixture onto two baking sheets and place in the preheated oven following the instructions on page 213.

- While the mini pie halves are baking, prepare the filling by beating the butter in a bowl until soft then gradually adding the icing sugar until the mixture is light and fluffy. Stir in the peppermint extract and green food colouring (if using) until fully incorporated.

- When the mini pie halves are cooked, leave them on the baking sheets for 5 minutes then remove with a metal spatula and place on a wire rack to cool. Once cooled, spread a rounded teaspoon of the creamy filling on the flat side of one pie half and sandwich together with another.

PEANUT BUTTER WHOOPIES

Follow the original whoopie recipe but sandwich the pie halves together with this nutty frosting.

MAKES 16 WHOOPIE PIES

1 X QUANTITY OF BASIC WHOOPIE PIE MIXTURE (SEE PAGE 213)

FILLING

1 TBSP MILK

110G (4OZ) BUTTER, SOFTENED

150G (5OZ) SMOOTH PEANUT BUTTER

225G (8OZ) ICING SUGAR, SIFTED

- Spoon the whoopie pie mixture onto two baking sheets and place in the preheated oven following the instructions on page 213.

- While the mini pie halves are baking, prepare the filling by beating the milk, butter and peanut butter together in a bowl until creamy then gradually adding the icing sugar until the mixture is light and fluffy.

- When the mini pie halves are cooked, leave them on the baking sheets for 5 minutes then remove with a metal spatula and place on a wire rack to cool. Once cooled, spread a rounded teaspoon of the creamy filling on the flat side of one pie half and sandwich together with another.

Blondie Whoopies

By dropping the cocoa powder from the original whoopie recipe (page 213) and substituting it with flour, you are left with really beautiful pale whoopie discs. I love to sandwich them together with a gorgeous white chocolate frosting.

MAKES 16 WHOOPIE PIES

345G (12OZ) PLAIN FLOUR

1 TSP BAKING POWDER

A PINCH OF SALT

190G (6½OZ) CASTER SUGAR

120G (4½OZ) BUTTER, SOFTENED

2 EGGS, LIGHTLY BEATEN

1 TSP VANILLA EXTRACT

250ML (8½FL OZ) BUTTERMILK

FILLING

110G (4OZ) GOOD-QUALITY WHITE CHOCOLATE, BROKEN INTO PIECES

1 TBSP MILK

175G (6OZ) BUTTER, SOFTENED

250G (9OZ) ICING SUGAR, SIFTED

- Preheat the oven to 180°C (350°F), Gas mark 4 and line two baking sheets with baking parchment.

- Sift the flour, baking powder and salt into a bowl. In another bowl, using a hand-held electric mixer, cream the sugar and butter together until pale and fluffy. Gradually add the eggs, mixing well to combine.

- Add the vanilla extract to the buttermilk and, alternating with the dry ingredients, add to the creamed butter mixture, mixing until everything is combined and you are left with a thick batter.

- Spoon 32 rounded teaspoons of the batter onto the prepared baking sheets, allowing about 5cm (2in) of space for them to spread while cooking. Bake in the oven for about 15 minutes until the tops have puffed up and spring back when lightly pressed.

- While the pie halves are baking, make the filling. Melt the white chocolate in a heatproof bowl set over a pan of gently simmering water (making sure the base of the bowl doesn't touch the water), stirring occasionally, until the chocolate is silky smooth. Remove from the heat.

- Beat the milk and butter in a bowl until creamy then gradually add the icing sugar until the mixture is light and fluffy. Stir in the melted white chocolate.

- When the mini pie halves are cooked, leave them on the baking sheets for 5 minutes then remove with a metal spatula and place on a wire rack to cool. Once cooled, spread a rounded teaspoon of the creamy filling on the flat side of one pie half and sandwich together with another.

Mega Chocolate and Pistachio Meringues

These meringues absolutely rock! They are crisp on the outside with a perfect marshmallow centre, and have chocolate and pistachio dust swirled right through . . . Meringues can be a bit scary if you haven't made them before but this recipe is fairly foolproof if you stick to it.

MAKES 6 MEGA MERINGUES

250G (9OZ) ICING SUGAR, SIFTED

4 LARGE EGG WHITES

2 TSP CORNFLOUR, SIFTED

1 TSP WHITE WINE VINEGAR

100G (3½OZ) GOOD-QUALITY DARK CHOCOLATE, FINELY CHOPPED

100G (3½OZ) PISTACHIO NUTS, FINELY CHOPPED

WHIPPED CREAM, TO SERVE

- Preheat the oven to 150°C (300°F), Gas mark 2 and line two baking trays with baking parchment.

- Draw three 12cm (4¾in) circles on each piece of parchment. Then turn the parchment over so your meringues don't end up with pencil marks on them.

- In a stand-alone mixer or using a hand-held electric mixer, whisk the icing sugar and egg whites together on high for 10 minutes until glossy white peaks form. Using a spatula, fold in the cornflour and vinegar, then gently fold in the chocolate and pistachios.

- Divide the meringue mixture between the circles pencilled on the parchment and, using a tablespoon, swirl the mixture to form six equal-sized meringue discs. Bake in the oven for 45 minutes, then remove from the oven and allow to cool completely. Enjoy with large dollops of freshly whipped cream.

JULGRÖT A.K.A. CINNAMON RICE PUDDING

This dessert will always remind me of Christmas. I picked this recipe up in Sweden, where they make big batches of it around the festive season (*jul* means 'Christmas' in Swedish). It's fairly filling, but once in a while, a big bowl of rice pudding can be extremely comforting.

SERVES 4

200G (7OZ) PEARL RICE (PUDDING RICE)

A PINCH OF SALT

1 TBSP BUTTER

1 LITRE (1¾ PINTS) FULL-FAT MILK

4 TBSP VANILLA SUGAR (SEE PAGE 195), PLUS EXTRA TO SERVE

½ TSP GROUND CINNAMON, PLUS EXTRA TO SERVE

WHIPPED CREAM, TO SERVE

○ Add the rice, 250ml (8½fl oz) of water and the salt and butter to a large saucepan, then cover with a lid and place over a high heat. Bring to the boil then reduce the heat and simmer for 10 minutes until the water has been absorbed and the rice is cooked.

○ Pour in the milk and add the vanilla sugar and cinnamon. Stir through to combine then bring to the boil again. Reduce the heat and simmer slowly for 25–35 minutes until you have a creamy consistency but the rice still has a little bite to it.

○ Pour the rice pudding into a baking dish and allow to cool before covering and popping it in the fridge until chilled.

○ Serve big hearty spoonfuls of the chilled rice with an extra sprinkling of vanilla sugar and cinnamon and big dollops of whipped cream.

INDEX

ACKNOWLEDGEMENTS

To the queen of the puns and my pal, Jenny Heller, who swanned into my life dressed to the nines, I am so glad you didn't take one look at the young fella sitting in the café in Dublin and run a mile. Thanks for all the inspiration, encouragement and advice; can we retire yet? My fantastic and highly efficient editor Ione Walder had no problem dragging me from one deadline to another with soldier-like productivity and of course a fantastic sense of humour, and is by the way one of the best tour guides in London. A massive thanks to Elen Jones, to Myfanwy Vernon-Hunt for the absolutely stunning layouts, and of course to the lovely Lee Motley and Selina Juneja for the beautiful cover designs.

To my two main ladies Lucy Jessop and Charlie Clapp (both big fans of bangers and mash), thank you so much for all the hard work cooking and styling the food for the photos in the book. Many hilarious hours were spent by us all in the corner of Plough Studios during a long hot summer in London, but I hope you'll all agree that it was worth it for the fantastic and delicious images that were the result. My prop hero, Jo Harris, never ceased to amaze me by turning up with boxes upon boxes of the most stunning props for the food photos; despite all my threats to rob them, I never did! Massive respect for anyone who can keep track of hundreds and hundreds of random pieces of kitchenalia.

Thanks to the main man and über-photographer Chris Terry, for the long day spent shooting photos in the most amazing kitchen in London. Chris shot the amazing cover for the book and this fella has absolutely no shortage of energy!

Massive thanks to James Byrne, who put his neck on the line and took a chance when he flew over to Dublin and spent a weekend shooting images with me. Very few people have seen me fishing (James is now one of them) and there is a good reason: I am not at my most manly when squealing like a young lady whilst trying to pick up a floundering mackerel. James, you keep that story to yourself!

My food-styling, recipe-testing godmother, Erica Ryan, spent hours upon hours cooking up a storm from the recipes in the book. For the constant helping hand, a big *big* thank you.

A big thank you also to David Hare, for having your finger on the button and picking up the phone to organise a meeting, after hearing me on the radio. Thanks for the constant advice and support and for listening to all my wild ideas for the TV show. A big thank you also to Brian Walsh at RTE for taking a chance on me.

My long-suffering parents, despite my interesting combination of friendly abuse and love, continue to offer non-stop support, love, and advice and an endless supply of fresh fruit and veg. To my mom, no one throws a herb pot like you – the real kitchen hero. She kept us all well-fed every day while we were growing up, and entertained us with her fantastic sense of humour. And thanks to my dad for the great sense of adventure, work spirit and mischief that came hand in hand with growing up in the Skehan household! Also a big thank you to my grandparents, Chris and Betty, who are full of inspiration, stories and non-stop support.

A massive thank you to my many family members for all the amazing support and for constantly recommending the blog and books to people. You're the best PR team I could ever have wished for!

To my long-suffering pals Jonathan, Comedy Paul, Catriona, Kate, Aoife, Daragh, Suzanne, Brian, Laura and Simon, thanks for sitting patiently through all the filming and eating on cue, plus the many other random things I've asked you to do over the years.

And last but not least, to my beautiful Sofie, who is there through it all: the highs, the lows and the in-betweens; thanks for putting up with me *älskling*!

First published in 2011 by Collins
an imprint of HarperCollins *Publishers*
77–85 Fulham Palace Road
London W6 8JB

www.harpercollins.co.uk

10 9 8 7 6 5 4 3 2

Publishing Director: Jenny Heller
Editorial: Ione Walder
Design: Myfanwy Vernon-Hunt
Food Styling: Lucy Jessop
Prop Styling: Jo Harris

The *Kitchen Hero* TV series was produced by Inproduction Ltd.
*Inproduction.**TV**

A catalogue record for this book is available from the British Library.

ISBN: 978-0-00-738302-3

Printed and bound in Spain by Graficas Estella